UNCUT GUIDE TO AN AMAZINGLY SUCCESSFUL CAREER IN BARBERING

HASHEEM WHITMORE

Printed in the United States of America

ETERNAL PUBLISHING
SACRAMENTO, U. S. A.

THE UNCUT GUIDE TO AN AMAZINGLY SUCCESSFUL CAREER IN BARBERING.
Copyright © 2015 by Eternal Publications. All rights reserved. No part of this publication may be reproduced, stored in a retrieval system, or transmitted, in any form or by any means, electronic, mechanical, photocopying, recording, or otherwise, without the prior written permission of the copyright owner except in the case of brief quotations embodied in critical articles and review. Reprint and return information address Eternal Publications, c/o 5350 Dunlay Drive, Unit 916, Sacramento, California 95835.

ISBN 13: 978-0-9969205-0-6
ISBN 10: 0996920501

LIBRARY OF CONGRESS CATALOG CARD NUMBER 2015917217

This book is dedicated to you.

(Go ahead smile; it is really dedicated to you. It was about time.)

Prologue

Congratulations on your purchase of this book. Its purpose is to educate and inspire the next generation of men and women who aspire to earn the title of Barber. Barbers have the amazing ability to influence the lives of everyone that sits in their chair. My success in life has been the result of four amazing barbers to whom I owe endless amounts of praise, for they are the ones who instilled principles of success into my life.

To Eddy Feggins,
My Personal Barber,
The consistent joy that you showed every time you cut my hair, along with your honesty and professionalism was great motivation to a 12-year old boy who was being raised by a single mother and had a distant father whose actions and words were nightmarish and destructive to his confidence. Thank you for being extremely positive in my life.

Thank you for listening to stories of my first kiss, countless homecoming dances, getting my driver's license, losing my virginity, keeping my grades up when I was falling off, helping me forgive people who hurt me, helping my mother when she had alopecia by fading her hair so it was not noticeable. Thank you for being honest and treating people fairly. Thank you for cutting my hair at times when we had no money to pay you. You shared your life with me and when you retired, I knew I was destined to one day be a man like you.

To Mr. Bryant Fletcher,
My Barber Instructor and Friend,

Thank you for seeing so much strength in me, even when I had lost faith in myself. I remember our first chat was on your second day of teaching and my third day of being in school. I received a call, at break time from my job as a security guard and was fired. Emotionally, I stood in front of you as a stranger worried and scared about quitting barber school because I had no way to support myself, and you told me things were going to get better, you said that with so much confidence that I believed it. From that moment on, I believed in myself that things were going to get better and nothing was going to stop me.

You told me to always stay focused on what I was doing. You taught me how to use the power of words to encourage people rather than cut at them and kill their spirit. I recall wondering why you would let students cut and butcher your hair and you would walk around proudly rather than fix it, you told me it was more important to be supportive of the students' efforts and dreams than to hurt them by fixing it. You taught me to be direct and not to fear confrontation. I remember our last conversation; I shared with you my success which was once just a dream, and we planned on you visiting California to see. The next day you were gone. A motorcycle accident. Though I was sad that you were gone; I rejoiced that you left this earth doing something you loved.

To Russell Roy,
Owner of the first ever barbershop I worked at, while still in barber school,
Thank you for giving me a chance, you allowed me to work rent free in your shop. You taught me that my chair was my pulpit, that only what I have in me is that which I can give to my clients, and it was important that I be positive.

You taught me about setting short achievable goals, and how before long I will have everything that I want. You and your family became my family when you celebrated and encouraged me when I won the "Barber of The Year" title in my first competition for barbering. The cake and ice cream you sent when I got my barbers license, even my blood family didn't do that much. You offered your home to me when I was on the verge of being homeless. Most importantly, you taught me to believe, and since then I have believed in myself, my abilities, and others because of what you taught me. I pray that one day, my words and work inspires another person to dream enormously big.

To Chuka Torres,
My friend, 'The Rich Barber',
Your active approach to life, business, and financial freedom for following your passion added gas to the pilot light that burned inside of me. The example and encouragement you gave me is something that I always strive to live and give. Thank you for introducing me to the laws of success and seeing the vision along with me for amazing success through giving. - *Rich for eternity, barbers till infinity.*

Special Thanks

Samuel and Cora, Rita, Dale, Jamaal, Robert, Kiel, Tamika, Danny, Shamise, Warren, Q, Vincent, Marcus, Arturo, Lucky, Laurie, Justus, Opal, Leon, Al, Alex
Also to every client whom has ever and will ever hold me as their Barber.

Table of Contents

Back Story 14
Personal Introduction 16
Love Your Craft 19
Barbering: A Short Introduction 23
    Barber School 25
    Being Clean 26
    Interning 26
    How to Get Paid 28
        Booth Rent 28
        Commission 29
        Salary 29
        $100,000.00 Annual Example 30
Insurance 31
Professional Barbering 33
    Professional Practise's 33
        Such Crustiness! 49
        The Exit 51
Equipment 53
    Tools 53
    Supplies 56
    Record Keeping 59
Managing Your Business 77
    Customer service 77
    Going Beyond Client Expectations 79
    Exceeding Expectations 80
    Example Conversation 81
    The Art of listening 85
    Become a Student of BODY LANGUAGES 86
        Micro Expressions 86
    Connecting with Clients 86
        Customer Expect 87
The Art of Handling People 89
    Ways to Making more Money 95

Marketing 101
UN Focused Approach 101
Referrals 102
Understanding Types of Clients...102
Appreciating 103
Popping By..104
Developing a Center of Influence..105
Community...109
Passing out Business Cards 112
Go to Community Events 113
Volunteer...113
Use Social Media 114
Use Fliers..114
Law of Retaliation 115
Own Your Niche..116
Become Part of your community 116
Community service 117
Gaining Success 120
Achieving Top Productivity 120
Personal Management 120
Time Management 120
Energy Management 120
Change What You Expect 121
Set Goals For 121
Important Income Considerations 124
Investing...127
STOCK, BONDS, TRUST And MORE..128
Creating a New Product or Labeling an Existing Product 133
Creating a Product..133
Licensing a Product 134
Reselling a Product...134
Difference between Broke and Poor 134
Facts about the Rich 134
Millionaires Top Ranking Success Factors 134

The Sequence for Personal Financial Success	135
The Sequence for Business Financial Success	136
Financial Assessment Guide	137
Staying Healthy	140
Mentally	140
Physically	141
Diet	141
Weight Loss	141
Meal Prep	144
List of Low Glycaemic Foods	144
Managing Fatigue and Aches	149
What Products Help	150
Neck Stiffness	150
Back Pain	153
Feet Strain	156
Hand Stiffness	158
Stretches	161
Cutting	182
Blade Theory	186
Fading	187
Blending	188
Beards	188
The Art of Lining	190
The End	193

PROLOGUE

"I am the Greatest, I said that even before I knew I was." Muhammad Ali

Back Story

I park my car, taking a few deep breaths and on out. By my third stride, I push the button to lock the car, having no time to look back. I have to be in and out within 15 minutes, otherwise mission fail. I am running too fast to be affected by the cold air whipping around Reagan National Airport in Washington D.C.

Passing all the happy faces at the baggage claim and food court, I wonder briefly what people think as they see a 22-year old six ft. tall black man running at full speed through the airport. I was trying to get to the bank to cash an unemployment check.

How did I get here? Few months earlier, I was living in San Diego, making good money as an insurance agent. Now I am 3000 miles from home, with no job, and an ex-girlfriend who cheated on me. My uncle that told me barbering was just a hustle which really hurt me, but what can you say when you are staying at his house, it hurt a lot. I dreamt that one day I would prove to myself, my love ones and all the people who did not have faith in me, those who did not believe that barbering was all I needed, they were all very wrong. I always felt that if I could just be the world's greatest barber to one person, like my barber was to me than I could live my life in the happiest and most meaningful way I saw fit.

In Barber College, I was broke, lonely, and stressed out yet I knew deep down that sometimes to achieve your dreams, you have to go through hell for it because it is worth finding out about yourself and knowing that you can be persistent in achieving whatever you want.

Three years later, I bought my first house while having an apartment as well, car, truck, and a motorcycle. A booming barbering business which had nothing to do with 'on the side' or illegal backing. Now Ten years later, my business is still growing and getting stronger. My life goal is to help the next generation of barbers succeed in this business. To dispel all the myths and the negative reasons that might be keeping them from putting all their efforts into what they are destined to do. Everything and everyone has a purpose and it is our job as humans to identify and pursue our purpose.

I know my purpose in life is to be a barber, and just like you, I was once doubtful about choosing barbering as a career, knowing that there was a passion that burned inside of me. I feel a great sense of achievement in transforming the way someone looks and feels about themselves. Being able to be desired for my skills and my positivity so much that people would want to sit in my chair for the rest of their lives and to me one day have someone say I owe a lot of my success to my barber who always encouraged me, and told me to never give up. Someone did that for me and that is why I wrote this book.

In the pages below, I give you the game. What they did not tell you in barber school, you will get it here. By the time you finish this book, you will be ready for a barber's life. You will learn how to run your business, grow your business, manage your money, and stay healthy too. I advise you to read this book multiple times because each time you read it, you will learn something new that you can start applying and sharing immediately. But before we get started allow me to introduce myself.

Personal Introduction

Hello, my name is Hasheem Whitmore. I am very happy you came by; I am always glad to see people here. I am many things: fighter, survivor, lover, friend, insightful adviser, mack, shark, go hard, wildest person at the party, push-to-the-limit and then some type of playa who loves people more than anything, but still has intimacy issues.

My parents divorced when I was 12 and shortly after I felt unimportant and devalued by my father. I was beat down emotionally. But unexpectedly, an unyielding source of support came into my life, in the form of a man named Eddie Feggins, my barber. Eddie was a cool ass old playa that had something I really needed to see; Happiness. Every time I got my hair cut by him he seemed to be on top of the world. My barber, not my father, was the one I talked to when school got stressful, when I got my driver's license, when I had my first heartbreak, when it was time to go to prom, and my plans for college. For years we discussed the importance of going against the odds and believing in yourself, the significance of having a vision, loving what you do, faith, parenting, patience, being open, forgiveness, and owning your own truth.

I owe my career and success to the man who created and inspired the man I came to be. I wanted to be happy, do something that I love, inspire and uplift others, motivate and encourage people to be their best, to love harder, fear nothing, and shake up the world. I got your back, dream big and then dream bigger, I am an always-in-your-corner type of man, who will put you back together when you are broken and need to feel that clean hair cut that comes with a renewed sense of positivity. I will lift you up with laughter, I will go to the abyss for you and if you need a prayer or two, you got it.

I am an individual who is getting better and better with each day passing. I have played the field a lot, learning more everyday about myself and having success and failures along the way. I have been blind (literally, I lost my vision for a short period of time when I was 11 years old), broken, burglarized, played, laughed at, pissed off, and counted out. But still, I rise every day to encourage someone to believe in themselves. I am the world's greatest barber because I love helping people feel good about themselves more than anyone else. I absolutely refuse to believe that it is too late for anyone to have the life they want.

Your time is now. Love, why don't you? Do you appreciate what is good in your life? Can you see it? Because I can see it for you. Destiny is knowing in your heart what you are intended to be, Faith is believing you will get there. You get back what you put in. As a licensed CA Barber, I love what I do for people. Giving a great haircut gives me great pleasure, but beyond that I try to constantly give more service, care, and encouragement to my clients, and by doing this I have been truly blessed.

This book is a lifetime of lessons, victories, mistakes, and proven principles and laws which if learned and applied, can transform fear into faith and mediocre into great. I hope you enjoy and apply these great principles into your life as much as I did learning and applying them in mine, because I had a ball. Welcome again.

GETTING STARTED

"You can do It if you Believe You Can!" Napoleon Hill

Love Your Craft

Love was put at the very first chapter of this book on barbering, because it is the most important thing you can have that will give you years of fulfilling experiences and separate you from the rest of the barbers and those who cut hair. Understand that there is a very big difference between some one that cuts hair and a barber. The former has a skill for cutting, may like cutting hair, and might be really good at it; sometimes these individuals' skills and ability can be the best in the shop. In the case of the former; cutting hair is a good way to make money for themselves but they fall short because what they're lacking is something you cannot teach and that is Love.

Love is the one thing that the world's greatest barber puts into everything he does for his career, his cuts, and his clients. People see and feel the difference between the two themselves. Understand that with life, what is in your heart will always prevail against whatever challenge presented. You will face different obstacles but what makes you great is that burning desire that you have what it takes to be the best.

The fact that you love making someone feel great about themselves is why you work so hard at giving them your best service. That is why you work so hard to learn new skills, buy new equipment, take the time to invest in yourself so you can be your best. When you care about each person that sits in your chair as if they were one of your loved ones, you will have no limits on where life can take you and there will be **no competition** for you because you love this barber life more than anything.

People might be more talented than you and that is just fine; they may even have more clients than you and that is still fine, but fix in your mind that no one is going to love this more than you. If you do that one thing you will be extremely successful, popular, and loved. The beautiful thing is you do not have to be perfect! Just be yourself, embrace your unique style and do not worry about what other people say. You are pursuing your dream and that is the most important thing you can ever do. In time your speed will increase, as will your clientele and income.

Know that it only takes one person to dramatically boost your business. One person that you give your best to can bring you more clientele than you can imagine. It has happened to me countless times because I love people and look to build a relationship with every person that sits in my chair. When you do so, people will feel that they are not just investing in a cut, they can get a cut anywhere but what they get from you is something worth driving across town for, or worth flying across the country for.

This love is why they invite you to their graduations and want you there at their weddings, why they ask you to come see them perform or compete because you were there supporting them through it all. Supporting, coaching, encouraging, and being honest with them all the way. The biggest reward you can have is being able to share this beautiful thing called life while being in someone's corner.

This goes beyond just cutting hair, it goes into the feeling you give someone. If you invest your efforts into providing a one-of-a- kind experience, your success will be limitless. That being said, this book was written to give you the tools to endure all the challenges that come with being a great barber, how to manage yourself and your success so that you will be able to share what you love with others as long as possible.

Winning fastest fade Competition in 2013

Winning Sacramento's Best Barbershop Competition 2011 Sacramento's Best Magazine

2004 Golden Scissors Competition- Barber of the Year, Best Beard, 2nd place Barber Creation

Barbering: A Short Introduction

Barbering has been around since ancient civilizations. Barbers have been around wherever there was hair to be cut. At one time, barbers were also dentist and surgeons because of their great skills in handling sharp instruments with precision.

It was a common practice to perform a procedure called 'Blood Letting'. When people were stricken with certain diseases, their blood was actually drained from them. After the procedure, white clothes used in the process were red stained by blood. These clothes would then be hung outside of the barbershop; these cloth strips then twirled together by being blown by the wind. It soon become a symbol of the barbershop, which later was turned into the barber pole.

The art of cutting hair is also known as tonsorial art.

Ways to Become a Barber

Barber school
Most states in the U.S.A require aspiring barbers to complete state mandated hours of technical and practical training (meaning that you have to read a text book and work on live customers or mannequins). The main objective of barber school is to instill sanitary practices to help you pass the state board exam.

Apprentice Programs
In most states, an aspiring barber attends a class one day a week and then accumulates his state required hours by actually working in a barbershop under a licensed barber (which is a great way to earn money and build clientele).

Caution
Make sure you practice good habits and know your options, not all barbers you start off working under are the ones you want to continue working for. It is better to know what your options are if you need to change mentors. Also make sure that you are being treated fairly, if something does not sound right, ask your instructor or another barber for their opinion.

Levels of Barbering

Instructor - Certain states have advance courses that license you to teach barbering.

Master Barber - Varies from state to state but is usually based on time vested into cutting hair.

Barber - An individual who has completed the required state criteria and passed the exam, permitting them to offer barbering services to the public

Barber Student - A currently enrolled student working to complete state required training

Apprentice Barber - An individual who works and learns the skill of barbering under a licensed barber.

Barber School

Putting in hundreds of hours to take the Test to get your license.

Finishing state required hours is the name of the game, what you do while completing those hours is your call. Bottom line, it is very unlikely that you will find a barber school that teaches you enough to be able to compete with a veteran barber, especially by the time you complete all your state required hours. It is possible for you to be terrible at cutting hair when you finish school and the institution to whom you paid thousands of dollars could care less how good you are. They are there to take your money and teach you for the state board exam. Swimming or sinking in success is up to you.

Success is a combination of beliefs, thoughts, and habits which are important to getting off to a strong start. Consider yourself lucky if you end up attending a good school which has clean facilities and helpful staff that keeps a good track of your hours.

First thing to look for when choosing a Barber School is making sure that the institution is accredited. There are a lot of fly-by-night schools run by slick talkers and hustlers who will take your hard earned money and have you thinking everything is on the up and up until one-day the state board comes in and shuts down the whole operation. They take your money, charge people for the haircuts you do, and never give you a penny, and then the state board tells that you have been taken and none of your hours spent count - so you are out the tuition you spent so much money on. Go on to your state board website, they'll have a current list of accredited schools to go through. Save yourself the jail time from an assault on the owner of some bootleg barber college.

Next check which institutions qualify for student loans. Trust me if coming up with 6 to 15 thousand dollars up front is challenging for you, take out the loan and get started! Some schools offer payment plans as well, so always check what options are available. There are also state funded programs for people who have been locked up at some time in their past so check with your local state agency to see what programs are available.

Book work (theory) is not glamorous at all, learning about different layers of the skin and scalp can be frustrating for someone who just wants to cut hair. Be a master of your craft and study it all, your time spent acquiring knowledge can save you a lot of trouble by allowing you to identify certain scalp conditions in your clients who may need to seek medical attention.

Being Clean

An important practice when learning barbering is to develop habits of good cleaning and sanitation. Dirty environments repel people, and it can even be very detrimental to your own health if you stay in an unclean environment.

Approach every hair cut or mannequin assignment as if you were doing it for the state board exam. By developing better work habits early in your career as a student you will be well prepared to pass your exam and enter the world as a licensed professional barber.

Tips
- *Label all your tools; I had tools stolen while at the school.*
- *If you borrow anything from a classmate, make sure to return it as soon as you finish.*
- *Practice your shear work. This will help you tremendously in the long run because it opens you up to an even more diverse clientele.*
- *Do not limit your focus, learn every technique from color to chemicals, eyebrows to manicures and pedicure.*

Interning

Check out high end shops, franchises, and neighborhood barbershops. I recommend shadowing for at least a day to see how big the difference in skill and business operations can be. Notice the difference in presentation and customer service and attention to detail and uniformity.

Understand that a great shave and a great hair cut is the same all over the globe. A barber can charge a high price for services regardless of environment. Sometimes, we fall into the trap that only in high-end shops you can command high-end prices for your services.

Yes, it can feel like an obstacle when you become integrated to a shop standard but as an independent contractor you set your price. Determine your services and what value you give to your clients, and then set your price.

You can set yourself apart by providing premium service at a premium value. Consider this concept thoroughly when deciding what type of barber and what type of shop you choose to work for. Some barbershops offer great training while others offer other great benefits.

www.betheworldsgreatestbarber.com for additional information

THE BUSINESS

"Change Your Focus From Making Money To Serving More People Makes The Money Come in." Robert Kiyosaki

How to Get Paid

When choosing the barbershop you want to work in, you need to know how the Barber industry is set up. An important thing about working is that you will be earning money, the owners of the shop will obviously want to be paid off your work. You can choose to pay them in one of three ways: commission, salary, or booth rental.

It is recommended that you check what sort of payment they want before agreeing for work.

Also, when looking for work, check with a CPA or Tax Specialist to see whether you can qualify for certain tax breaks.

Booth Rent

You can choose to rent booths at barbershops, and at the end of each week your booth rent is due, if you have it set aside already - you are good to go. Taking a little bit each day and setting it aside is the easiest way to soften the blow of paying out cash every week.

It is the nature of the business - being an independent contractor, you are effectively renting a 4x5 foot space of an establishment to conduct your **business**.

Please remember the most important part of the last sentence is that it is your **business**. Treat it as such, a business that is managed efficiently and effectively, in an environment that meets your standards. Throughout my writings I use the word crusty which sums up an undesirable situation, relationship, an environment. Make sure you stay away from crustiness as much as possible.

You are a valuable commodity to your clientele. Your work and character speaks volumes, and through your skills of a great barber; you will always be able to make money in whatever atmosphere you choose. Thus, when you decide which establishment you will be paying thousands of dollars to each year, make sure you are happy with your choice.

Know that owners of the establishment you will be working for will most likely only care about getting money from you every week. They do not care if you had a single or a thousand cuts, they only want their rent. It is rarely the fault of the establishment or other barbers if you are struggling to make your rent. If it is not working for you, then you should work somewhere else.

Commission

Owner provides

- Electricity
- Workstation
- Compliance with State Standards set for Barber Establishment
- Receptionist*
- Client Data base*
- Education*
- W2* for tax purposes

* - denotes that service is optional

Benefits
Less concern over overhead cost but you lose some control over personal work times, break times, and work production depending on shop operating procedures.

Salary

- Barbers are expected to provide service to the public
- Practice State Standards of Sanitation
- Tools
- Complies with the rules and standards of the shop
- Take your hourly wages multiply by 2 and add three 0's to quickly see what you will make in a year. Example **$15 per hour x 2= 30 add ,000= $30,000 per year**

Benefits
You receive a set amount no matter if you cut 1 head per hour or 5.

$100,000.00 Annual Example

$100,000.00 = $8,400.00/month
$2,100/week
$416/day
$30/cut
14/cuts per day
1 ¾ haircut/per hour
8hr day

Caution
As a salary barber make sure you are being accounted for as an employee and not an independent contractor. Some owners want to treat you and pay you like an employee but treat you as an independent contractor when it comes to taxes, so they don't have to pay taxes that benefits you, such as workers' compensation.

Consult a tax professional for guidelines, laws and additional information.

Negotiate
Most things in life are negotiable, terms of the agreement are most important!

Know your math
Have a good understanding on the price of services you provide and how much you walk away with.

Don't forget to account for taxes. Consult a tax professional so everything is accounted for.

Truth
Know your worth. Make sure you get paid for what you are worth. In this industry you are going to pay a % of your earnings to a shop owner if you choose to work in an establishment.

Analyze the situation carefully and choose the best environment. Often, salary-offering shop owners have a stronger influence over barbers. This means more rules. They keep track of how much you are making, and expect extraordinary standards, because the more you earn, the more they earn.

Insurance

Liability Insurance:

Any type of insurance policy that protects an individual or business from the risk that they may be sued and held legally liable for something such as malpractice, injury or negligence. Liability insurance policies cover both legal costs and any legal payouts for which the insured would be responsible if found legally liable. Intentional damage and contractual liabilities are typically not covered in these types of policies.

Professional Liability:

Insurance that protects professionals such as accountants, lawyers and physicians against negligence and other claims initiated by their clients. It is required by professionals who have expertise in a specific area because general liability insurance policies do not offer protection against claims arising out of business or professional practices such as negligence, malpractice or misrepresentation.

Tip

Liability insurance protects you! You never know when you might accidentally cut someone. Don't tell everyone you have insurance, just get it and pray you never have to use it.

Commercial General Liability:

A type of insurance policy that provides coverage to a business for bodily injury, personal injury, and property damage caused by the business' operations, products, or injury that occurs on the business' premises. Commercial general liability, or CGL, is considered comprehensive business insurance, though it does not cover all risks that a business may face.

Homeowners Insurance

A form of property insurance designed to protect an individual's home against damages to the house itself, or to possessions in the home. Homeowners insurance also provides liability coverage against accidents in the home or on the property.

Tip

Some homeowners or rental insurance policies protect personal possessions from theft away from the residence. Over your career you will spend a lot of money on equipment, therefore research different policies to make sure you cover your equipment.

Health Insurance

A type of insurance coverage that pays for medical and surgical expenses that are incurred by the insured. Health insurance can either reimburse the insured for expenses incurred from illness or injury or pay the care provider directly. Health insurance is often included in employer benefit packages as a means of enticing quality employees.

Medigap

Also called Medicare Supplement Insurance, Medigap is health insurance coverage provided by private companies designed to cover excess costs not covered by original Medicare.

Tip

As Barbers a lot of the time we have to provide ourselves with our own insurance coverage since we are often independent contractors. But we often overlook the importance of having a supplemental insurance that may cover additional medical bills or loss of earnings. Do your research and get covered for those times you can't physically cut due to injury or illness.

Business Automobile Policy - BAP

It is recommended that a company obtain a business automobile policy even if it does not own vehicles if its employees use personal vehicles for business purposes. In the event of a serious accident the employee may not have enough personal liability coverage to adequately protect the business.

Tip

If you have a mobile barbering business it is wise to check out what your personal automobile policy covers and not covers. Certain usage may require you to have a business automobile policy so check with your insurance professional.

Definitions @ | Investopedia http://www.investopedia.com

Injury and Work

Injuries are definitely possible in any work environment. A barbershop is no exception to it.

If you are working as an employee, then your relevant state's laws may offer work-accident compensation, where your employer will be responsible for giving you compensation pay until the doctor says you are fit to return working. A permanent disability, such as losing a hand, ear, or eye has other more detailed coverage. Consult your state laws for more information on workplace injuries insurance.

Keep in mind though that illnesses such as common cold or flu do not count as workplace injury and are not compensated through state laws.

However, if you are working as an independent contractor, then you may need to apply for secondary insurance coverage. Again, check your relevant state laws for further information.

Professional Barbering

Professional Practices

Build a Clientele: arrive at your shop earlier than everyone else by at least an hour. At closing time, stay later then everyone else by at least an hour.

Plan out your meals: A barber on an empty stomach can only go so long before hitting the wall.

Get plenty of rest: Sleep well during the night, fatigue always cuts into your ability to move faster and cut longer.

Exercise regularly: Though it might not appear physically demanding, overtime cutting all day can take its toll on you. I have had back pain which I was able to eliminate by developing a stronger core. Leg pain which I was able to eliminate by taking breaks, stretching and doing lower body exercises such as squats and calf raises.

Get Supportive footwear

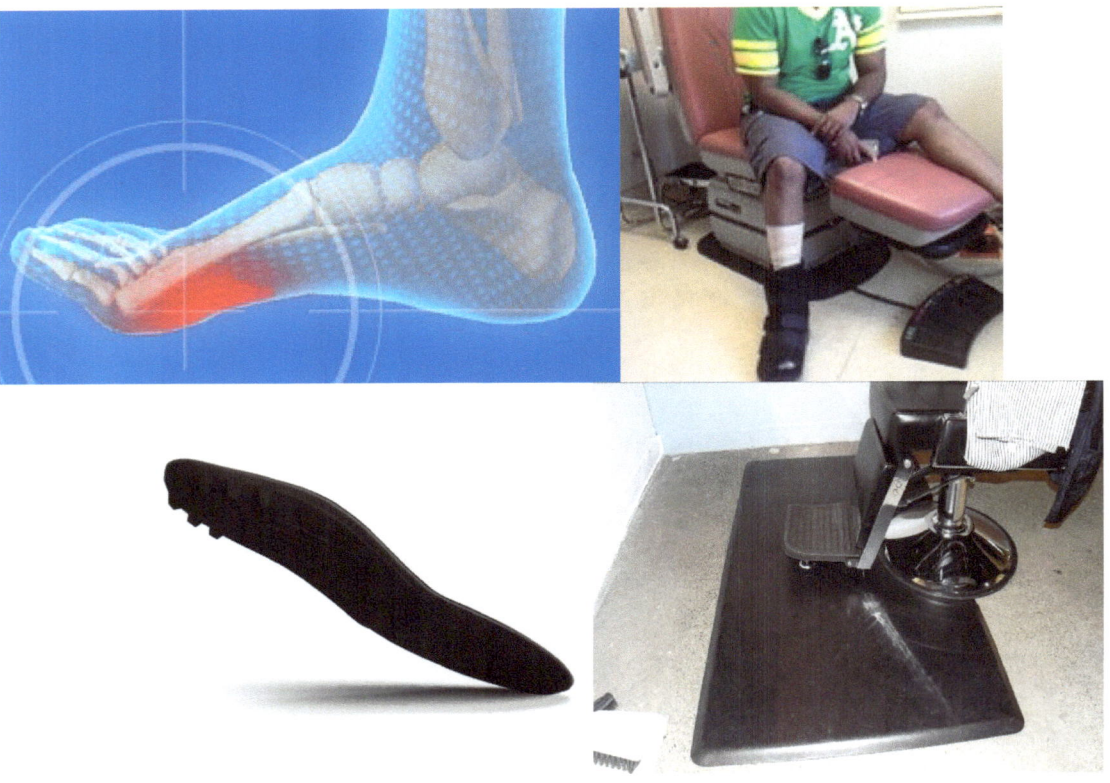

Get comfortable, supportive footwear and invest in a good quality anti-fatigue, do not go cheap!

I used to wear dress shoes and casual low tops to work, because of that I would have the occasional foot pain which I always ignored, till one day my foot swelled up like a fat person riding on a scooter at the grocery store; I had this jerking pain, my foot had endured all it could yet it was found to be fractured in three places. Avoid this happening to you, get good shoes and insoles to go on your feet.

Systems

Successful barbering businesses are built upon good systems. A system is a standard way of doing something the same way every time and getting a consistent and predictable result.

In this chapter you will learn:
Barbering requires you to build a brand. Your own personal brand is being built from the moment you start cutting hair. People you've never met will know about you, your service and your work ethic. Know that word travels fast about you everything from your skills at cutting to whom you may be dating will circulate in your community. As social media advances and clients have the ability to instantly post reviews about you or your service and your shop:

*How having systems for you affects your client's experience.
*Why you need systems.
*What areas of business requires systems.

THIS IS HOW IT WORKS:

A client comes to you for a cut. You know this is your opportunity to win another possible life time client. So you give them your best service. You break out a fresh clean drape, use your best manners, and even offer them a refreshing beverage. Your consultation is professional, attentive and thorough. Your focus is completely engaged on your client experience. You blow your client away with your service; after leaving the shop all they are thinking is *"Wow, I think I just found my Barber."* The professional service you give is great; your customer service was outstanding! But the service, the service was amazing! They want to tell everyone about how great you shampoo. They'll rave about the pleasing scents of the oil you use to exfoliate their skin in the hot towels you put on their face. They'll steal glances of themselves every chance they get to look at how good their hair looks; think about how masterfully you used your shears. They'll brag about how you used the straight razor to give them the closest shave, precision line that they've ever had! They can't wait to get back into your chair.

HOW TO LOSE A CLIENT

Visit 1:

So know you think you got this person hooked on your service. The big tip you received, how the two of you exchanged contact information. The way they insisted you give them more cards so they can pass them out to their friends and family has you feeling confident.

Visit 2:

Things start slowly declining. You might be out of refreshments so you don't offer them anything. But everything else is stellar and lives up to your client's expectations aside from being a little thirsty, things are great.

Visit 3:

Still no refreshments, the haircut, shampoo, and shave still was great but this time you spent half the time talking over your client to the barber next to you, talking about everything from music, sex, politics, and business. Then the other fifty percent of the time you're on your cell phone. Hair cut looks great but something feels different to the client.

Visit 4:

Still no refreshments, no shampoo or hot towels today you where 20mins late getting him into the chair. And while he waited patiently you are showed no hustle to get him in the chair faster or no effort to make sure he was comfortable while he waited. You haven't been to the beauty supply to re-up on shampoo or razor blades, so again they won't get all the services they may be expecting. This time you use clippers and barley even use your shears. You use an electric shaver rather than a razor to give them a close shave. This time you spend 90% of the entire time on your phone. You even take a short smoke break in the middle of the cut. The hair cut is still great; but when the client leaves this time he knows that was the last time he was going to get cut by you!

TIP: *THIS WILL MAKE YOU MORE MONEY INSTANTLY SO REMEMBER THIS IS HERE. IF YOU ACKNOWLEDGE AND APPRECITIATE PEOPLE YOU WIN. AT OUR CORE WE WANT TO BE ACKNOWLEDGE AND APPRECIATED. ESPECIALLY WHEN PAYING FOR A SERVICE. THE MOMENT YOU STOP SHOWING THAT FOR YOUR CLIENTS THEY ARE GONE. THE MOMENT YOU DO FOR ALL PEOPLE YOU WILL DRAW AND KEEP MORE CLIENTS AND BE ABLE TO KEEP THEM FOR YEARS. WHEN THEY WALK INTO THE SHOP AND YOUR RUNNING BEHIND COMMUNICATE THAT IMMEDIATELY. AND APOLOGIZE FOR RUNNING BEHIND, SHOW CONCERN ABOUT THERE SCHEDULE AND THEIR TIME. TIME IS OUR MOST VALUABLE RESOURCE THE ONE THING WE CAN NEVER GET BACK. CHUKA ONCE TOLD ME "YOU CAN'T WASTE TIME." YOUR TIME ESPECIALLY AND DEFINITELY THE TIME OF OTHERS, WHEN IT COMES TO PEOPLE, BY SHOWING THAT YOU CARE ABOUT THEIR TIME THAT IS WASTED, WILL MAKE PEOPLE NOT MIND WAITING ON YOU. WE MIGHT NOT REMEMBER WHAT YOU SAID OR HOW GOOD OR BAD YOUR HAIRCUT WAS; BUT, WE WILL ALWAYS REMEMBER HOW YOU MADE US FEEL. LIFE IS A FEELING PROCESS, PEOPLE LEAVE OR STAY WITH BARBERS THAT THEY HAVE BEEN WITH FOR YEARS BECAUSE OF THE WAY THEY ARE MADE TO FEEL.*

What happened!?

People like going to a place where they can get satisfactory consistent service. By being consistent you give them the purchasing power to choose their experience. When you start changing the experience for whatever reason you take away their ability to choose the quality of service they expect, and are subjected to whatever you choose to do that day. People hate not knowing what to expect.

Systems help you be successful

Systems allow you to plan perform and execute to a standard that is consistently improving your business. Systems in place will help you keep adequate inventory and supply, track your income and expenses, Cut faster, and much more. Simply put you'll be doing the same routine actions in your business to ensure your success.

System: any formulated, regular, or special method or plan of procedure.

Business Standards

You have to have standards on how you perform every part of your barbering business.

The presence of Standards are prerequisites to working and achieving results

Barber Business System Roadmap

Three Essential Business Disciplines

Three Essential Business Processes

Seven Centers of Barber Business Attention

System Development Worksheet

System: Haircut

Goal: give same consistent service

Flow Chart:

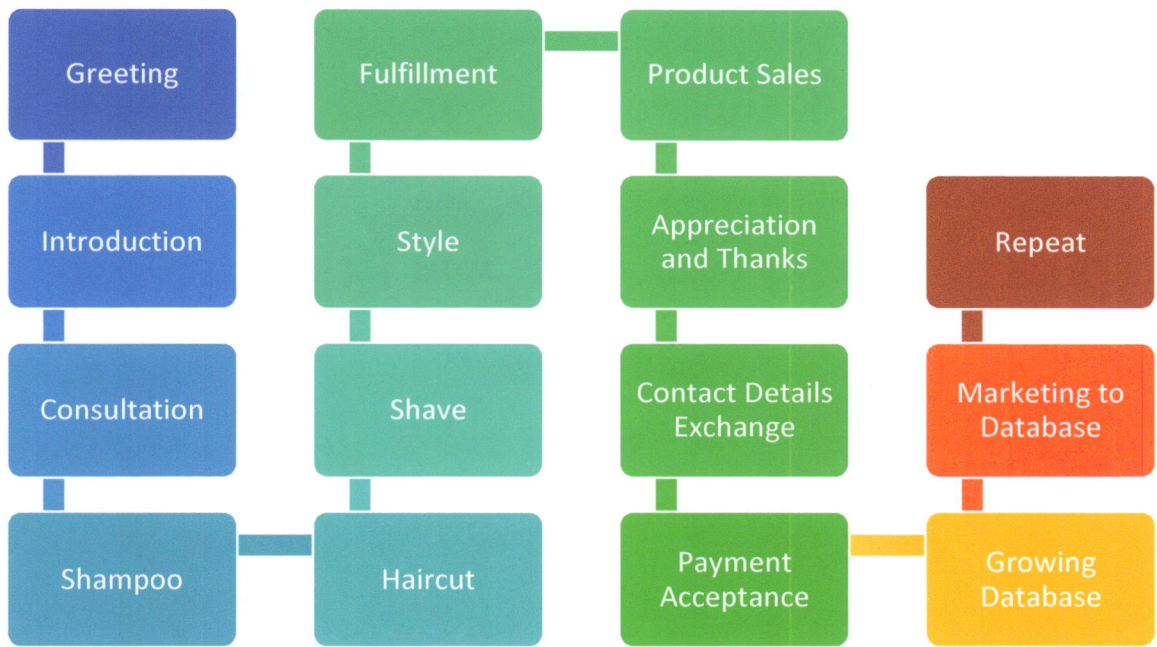

System Development Worksheet Sample

System: Marketing to Data Base

For each you will have systems of operation

- Thank you & Welcome E-Mail
- Making 5 Calls per Day
- E-Mail Clients at the 1st and 15th
- Visit Clients Every Week
- Hosting Annual or Semi-Annual Client Parties
- Creating Sales Funnel, auto responder and invoicing
- Sending Thank You Notes to Clients

KEYS TO SUCCESS

Remember your clients

This is a relationship business; anyone can cut hair, but a barber builds a relationship, take time to remember the people who pay your bills and invite you to their events.

Also try to remember one or two important things; "how is your dog doing?", "is your mother out of the hospital yet?"

When you greet people be happy to see them
.
Regardless if it is someone that comes to you, goes to another barber, or just a by passer. Have love towards people. If you are not that type of person, then you must pretend to be. Your attitude and outlook will draw people to you.

Can't make money off your chair while you are sitting on it!

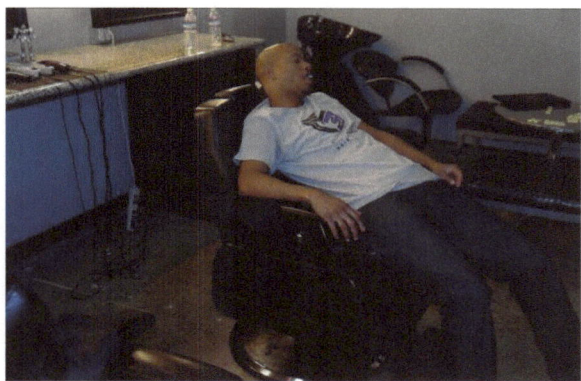

Stand behind your chair with a smile on your face. Show the world that you are ready to serve.

Pay attention to regulars that come into the shop that are not your clients.

Compliment the nice haircut they just received. This strengthens your bond with fellow co-workers. This makes it more likely that if ever they need a back-up barber, they may remember your decent attitude.

Trust me that the day will come when they will want to sit in your chair or bring a friend to try you out.

Never get butt hurt (offended) if a client goes to another barber.

If you continue to treat them with kindness and respect, they will never forget about your service. When they do return, give them your best service and ask for their recommendation on how you could improve your service.

Your humbleness will go a long way and you might even learn a valuable lesson on retaining your clients.

Ask clients what it was that drew them towards you

Ask what makes them keep coming back. Not only will this lead to a stroke of ego but can also be a great lead in asking them to refer you to their friends and relative.

Remember to be courteous.

Be nice, gentle, mannerly and courteous. Having good manners can go a long way in ensuring that your clients return to you again.

"Please sir/ma'am have a seat I am ready for you."
"Excuse me sir, would you mind if I answer the phone."
"Thank you for your patience."
"Thank you for coming, please come again."
"Would you like to schedule your next appointment today?"
"Thank you for giving me the chance to service you today."

These were just a few examples. Try to introduce courteousness in everything you do.

Keep your Shop and Station clean

At times when you are not cutting hair, get into the habit of cleaning everything from the windows to the walls. Having a clean workspace lets others know that you take pride in your environment. Most people will admire you for your cleanliness.

Wash your hands before every cut

Be especially vocal on letting your client know that you need a moment to sanitize and wash your hands. Do this consistently and your clients will be impressed by your cleanliness.

Limit phone calls you take during the cut

Phone calls take focus away from the most important thing – The client in the chair.

Only receive calls from someone already on your appointment book, even while in the middle of the cut. You never know they could be running late, bringing another person, or canceling. If the caller is not a client, call them back in between cuts.

Clients who want to talk will initiate deeper conversation

Feel free to tactfully engage in conversations. The key here is to get them talking about things that interest them. **Stay away from yes and no questions.** Ask them questions that take a couple sentences to answer.

Remember that when you are talking, you have to be cutting too. The problem that most barbers have is that once they start talking, their hand stop cutting and instead start gesturing. If you are going to be running your mouth, make extra sure to keep those clippers running!

Hygiene

Stinky body odor or bad breath can be offensive to people. Having a clean appearance and clean habits go very far.

Take Pride in Your Grooming Abilities

Snap before-and-after photos. Start building your catalog of great works you have performed.

Harmony in the shop

Harmony is when every barber in the building is on the same page of enjoying life, having some laughs, and getting money. Work hard to keep the balance of harmony. When you and your co-workers are having fun, more clientele comes through the door. People are entertained by how fun and lively everyone is and they often feel it the moment they step through the door.

When my friend and fellow barber in the shop thought that I had tried to make a move on his sister, the drama began. A small argument broke out between us in front of clients, who never came back. Even though we worked together every day, no words were spoken between us for about two years. Those two years were probably the hardest time for me and our clients, all of whom immediately noticed the difference in vibe.

The situation did not improve till almost two and a half years later. After a small incident, we actually talked and let the facts came out, mending the friendship and atmosphere of the shop. It is better to have a shop of two people working in harmony than to have two negative people killing the harmony of the shop.

Managing Down time

Shop downtime is the best time for advancements, if used properly.

Build clientele during downtime by talking to everyone that passes by, let people know that you are available to service them and their friends.

Visit nearby businesses, gain a rapport with the people that work close to you. Whenever they need to look fresh, they may send you clients from time to time.

Downtime is also a great opportunity to contact past clients. I usually start with clients that are about two weeks out since their last cut. A simple text asking how they are doing is good but try to ask something specific from your last encounter.

Start sending emails. They can be created within few hours and add value to your service. Including content that you write, or simply reference articles that can be helpful to your clients. These articles can be from any genre of your choosing. I like focusing on hair, upcoming events in the community, and product recommendations.

Downtime is also great for individuals who want to take online classes. I recommend trying to find a quiet place and using that time to log into your course and knock out some work. You will be amazed at how much work you can accomplish by working in short intervals.

Relax
Whenever we did not have any clients, we would play some sort of game; dominoes, pool, chess or some video games. Playing allows you to relax, rest your mind and body before the next wave of clients come in.

Knowing the time to call it a day

By Afternoon, the mental and physical fatigue starts to set in. The thought of grinding it out for one more client tickles your cerebral cortex. Your mind can picture five, maybe ten more cuts if you just push yourself a little more. You can feel the money stacking up in your pockets, if you just ignore the creeping pain in your feet or the tightness in your back, the dull pain in your shoulders and neck or the stiffness in your hands; bills can get paid, and clients will be happy you took care of them.

Why not? You can always rest when you are dead. Start stacking up money, grind the wheels till you fall off. If you don't cut them today do you know what might happen? They may find another barber and never come back! They may think that you do not value them. You may not have any clients tomorrow and then how will you pay your bills? All these concerns swirl around your head making so much noise that you debate sacrificing your body for money. But is it really money? Its fear, which is at the very root of most questionable decisions, just like the one you are contemplating.

Fear can be very damaging, especially when you are not honest with yourself about it. Fear of becoming broke, or not having extra money, pushed me in to adopting a Super Man complex so to speak. Telling myself that I could cut more hours than anyone else. My cuts will be superior to any other barber. I would move faster than anyone has seen. I would not waste valuable work time eating and taking breaks. I would eat a large breakfast in the morning and eat nothing afterward, so I could avoid the restroom breaks. I only drank small amounts of fluids so I could reduce the time running to the restroom, and avoid anything else that took away from cutting hair.

Looking back, I realize my own foolishness. But my vision of having this large clientele that loved my service soon filled up the shop and gave me the income to buy motorcycles, trucks, and my first home. I used to tell myself that the reason I push so hard is because I love cutting hair and feel great of such success.

I found out that if you push anything to the limit consistently, eventually the strain you put on yourself will start to break you down.

I remember standing at the urinal each day for my end of the day release; which was usually a very long event because I had so much built up, my bladder would be beyond full. Of course, I could not see any problem in this routine. Till one day, I returned to a waiting client after finishing my daily release. But my bladder was still releasing, Drip-Drip-Drip, and I could feel the moisture accumulating. I went back to the restroom and noticed that I could no longer control the flow. Literally, I tried to shake it off and get back to work. Dumb decision. But I had to get that money, I told myself. And off I went back to cutting, ignoring the warning sign that something was wrong.

Success mistake #2 came about three years later. I love looking nice and dressing nice, I spent years being overweight and I was very happy that after years of hard work I was able to lose 95lbs through exercise and eating better. But years of standing on my feet, wearing shoes that were stylish and lacking support, I would occasionally have sharp pain in my feet, which would usually last for a few days. I used to apply a lot of ice and ibuprofen to alleviate the pain at night, which always got me through the next day and that was my routine.

Superman could not afford to be off his feet and neither could I, so I consistently pushed through the pain, yet another dumb move! Then it finally happened during my tenth year of barbering, I had pushed through the pain all day while cutting hair, and each step I would take had become more painful than the proceeding one. It felt like each step was equivalent of jumping off a roof and landing barefoot on your feet. But I made it through the day.

Laying in my bed that night, I kept tossing and turning because my right foot burned as if though it was on fire. Eventually, I had to get up and go to the bathroom across the hall. As soon as my foot touched the ground, the pain erupted, my foot had swollen more than I had ever seen before. My once slim ankle more closely resembled the ankle of someone three times my size. I began sweating profusely and was on the verge of crying due to the pain. I tried limping towards the bathroom, but failed. I had to abandon that goal.

I cried out for help, my mother wrapped my foot with all the ice packs we had in the house. Later she wheeled me into the restroom in our computer chair and I finally relieved myself. I knew that after years of saying "I am going to work and grind till wheels fall off", my wheel had finally fallen off. I spent the next three months in an orthopedic boot with my foot up in the air; my foot was fractured in three different places because of the years of stress I put on them. While my other foot suffered from degenerative bone loss.

I want you to understand that the world will not fall apart if you take a break, call it an early day or take a **vacation**. Yes, someone might be unhappy or disappointed that they could not get a haircut, but you will never be able to please everyone, that is a fact.

You have to consider the big picture; the time you spend taking care of yourself will extend the years you will be able to consistently perform at older ages. If you listen to your body, make wise nutritional decisions, rest mentally and physically, and acquire the proper support equipment, such as well cushioned shoes with sturdy insoles, anti-fatigue mat, back and wrist braces and other equipment that provide great support during work.

See my list of great products @ www.betheworldsgreatestbarber.com

Such Crustiness!

Crusty: That which is undesirable or below your standards.

The shop you work at is the environment that you spend much of your daily life in, thus it is important the place is desirable and up to your standards. If you feel that the place is crusty, not working for you, and you feel that you can do better, then be confident and move on. Leave that crustiness in the past. Life is too short to live in crustiness.

After almost eight years of working in a barbershop in the hood, the decline was evident. Crack heads visiting frequently, hustling men in and out consistently, the writing was clearly on the wall. As a side note, whatever that is loitering around you is the direct reflection of what is going on in your shop.

If you see Eskimos there is probably an igloo somewhere around. If there are a bunch of crack heads coming into the shop, it means somewhere someone has some crack for them. If you ever come to that realization, leave that shop immediately. Because when the cops come in everyone is going down.

When the beef in the streets makes its way into your shop, you may end on the news as a witness or victim of a barbershop shooting. It happens. I advise you to always get contact info from all your clients (cell numbers, e-mail address) just in case you ever need to move shop, this way you can keep most of your clients. Know that when you leave a shop - do not - I repeat, do not expect your past co-workers to tell your clientele where you moved to. You are responsible for keeping contact with your clientele.

Warning signs

It's commonplace that when things are about to start sliding down hill, you will over hear shop owners complain about bills and utilities. Keep your ears open to this, owners ranting about electric and water bills, it may mean that they are about to increase your booth rent.

In some cases, the owner may even stop paying the bills, meaning that lights get turned off during the work hours. When this happens, make up your next move and start packing because owners can get very funny acting.

Use the Grandma Test

If your grandmother was to come visit the shop at any time; Would she feel safe? Would she say that it was clean? Would she feel comfortable? If the answer is 'No' then you should not be there either.

Make sure facilities such as bathrooms, sink and overall cleanliness is kept up.

For weeks I was working at a shop that had terrible standards of cleanliness. The toilet was constantly overflowing and even though we were located next to a known plumber shop, the owner did not want to invest in a professional solution. One day, we noticed a lot of little fruit flies flying around the shop. These aggressive little gnats were landing on clients' faces and being an annoyance. After around three or so weeks, I made an observation, I thought they were young flies and had to have a source somewhere in the bathroom. Turns out that the garbage had not been emptied in months, the trash can was full of maggots and larva whose eggs were hatching into the little flies infesting the shop.

Never speak badly about other barbers or clients

The barbering industry is a very small circle, and as the years go on it is getting smaller and smaller. Clients will step into the shop and share their traumatic experiences and tragedies at other barber shops. They will engage you in conversation in attempt to get you to bite on the negativity. DO NOT BITE.

Word will spread that you were talking negative, and at some point those words you put out there will come back. Clients will go back and forth between barbershops and give you a reputation for insulting and disrespecting others.

You never want to encourage or welcome drama as a barber.

You are easy to reach. People know all about you; your name, your car, where you work etc. You work in a public space and almost always have clients present. A person who wants to harm you can call and schedule an appointment with you, knowing that you will be there. Not a good situation to be in.

Remember to always practice safety.

When closing the shop, make sure that some friend or co-worker is there with you. Robbers see tired barbers as easy targets, because their pockets are full of cash after each day.

Never speak badly or share intimate details of clients

It is insulting or degrading to other clients. First, it reflects poor character. Second, it dissolves any trust that the next client may have on, what guarantee do they have that you will not share their details? Down talking is the perfect way to lose clients.

Exhibit your Work to others

Now remember when you are in the shop, every client in the shop is observing everything you do. You have the opportunity to get cut in front of an audience show off your work.

Start with detailing the beard first by providing a great shave or trim, the face is what people observe most. By having him with a clean face first, you quickly get him looking very sharp and people get to see your work the entire cut time rather than doing the beard last.

Once you get a particular side blended well turn that side to the waiting area and work on the other side. Keep checking your work in the mirror.

Remember this cut is your advertisement as well.

The Exit

Tips and Rules to leaving the Shop

1. Do on to others as you would have them do on to you. Make sure that you that give sufficient notice to employers that you are moving on to other opportunities. Keep your karma right and try not to burn any bridges. You never know what the future may hold. Twice I have left a shop without giving notice; one because of drug activity, for which I suggest that if you witness questionable behavior get the hell out of there. Second time the owner was an ass towards me, along with having some pretty questionable behavior. I decided it would be best to throw the peace sign and bounce. I also left two shops with adequate notice, and both times I was given a meal and well wishes.

2. Client List. You should be constantly in the practice of gathering information of your clients. Emails and Telephone numbers. That way when you leave, you will have means to get clients to your new location.

3. Your former co-workers will not tell your clients about your new location, do not expect them to either. There is no point in getting mad or sour because such is part of the game.

4. Definitely expect them to send over their extremely difficult clients to you.

5. Use social media to market your new shop and your new service.

6. Do not slander or talk shit about your last shop or co-workers. Negative words travel very fast so make sure that you keep negative comments to yourself and hold yourself to a higher standard. If people keep asking

about why you moved, tell them the change was for a better opportunity.

7. No one has the power to read your mind so keep an honest dialog with people.

8. No need for conflict. I have seen sour owners yell, scream, threaten, dare, curse, and a lot more when a barber leaves, because they feel played. Just say your peace, thank them for the opportunity and move on.

9. Promote, promote, and promote. Get on the ball of using which ever form of marketing you feel comfortable with; emails, passing out cards, having a health education day, have a party, volunteer. Create a buzz of exposure about your good service and good will and you will always have clients.

10. Keep note of clients who follow you everywhere. That is your inner circle of best clients. Offer them special events, promotions, coupons, thank you cards, and other ways you can appreciate them. Your core group is your most beneficial source of clients.

11. Stay positive, change brings about the unexpected. Know that there will be a brand new set of issues and problems that you will have to learn and adjust to. Be positive and believe in yourself. Stay on your grind and you will have the success you desire.

Equipment

Tools

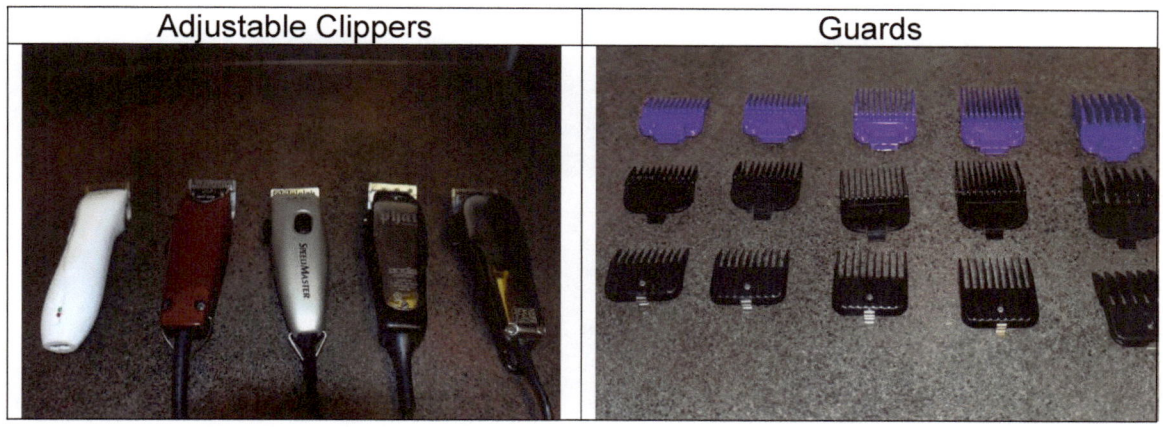

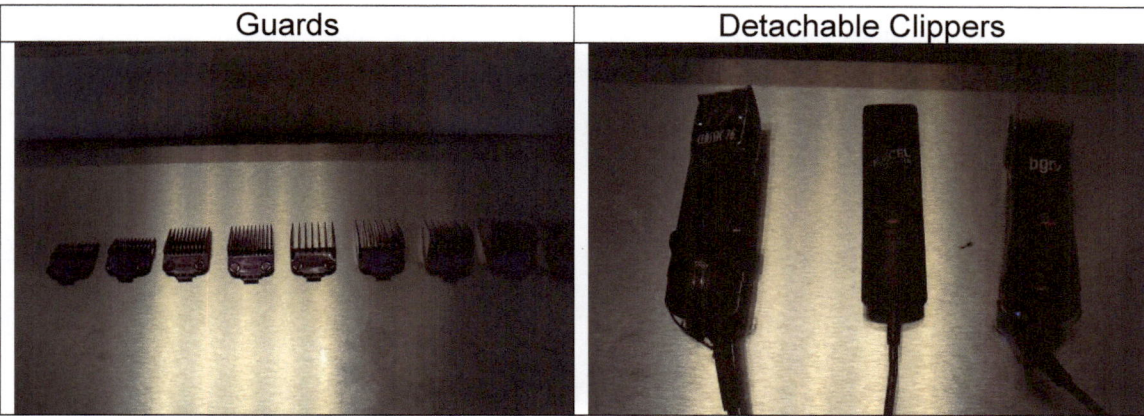

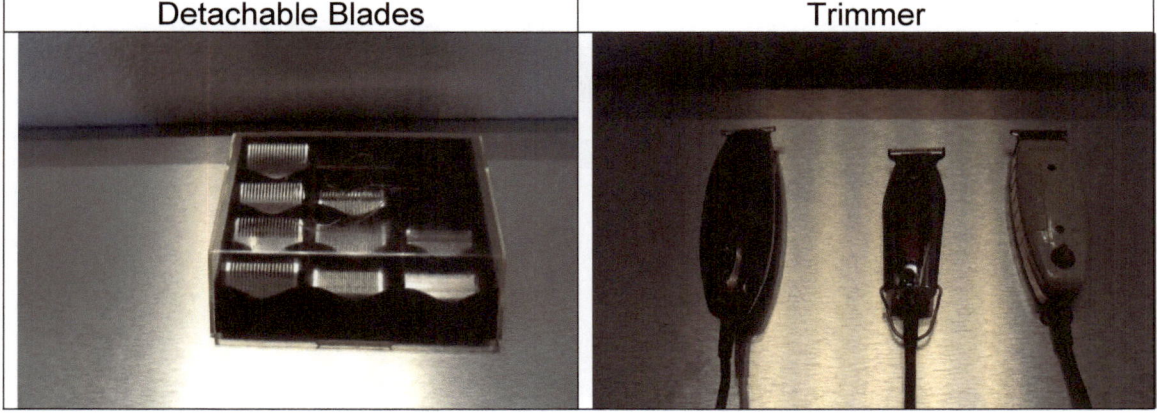

Shears	Thinning Shear
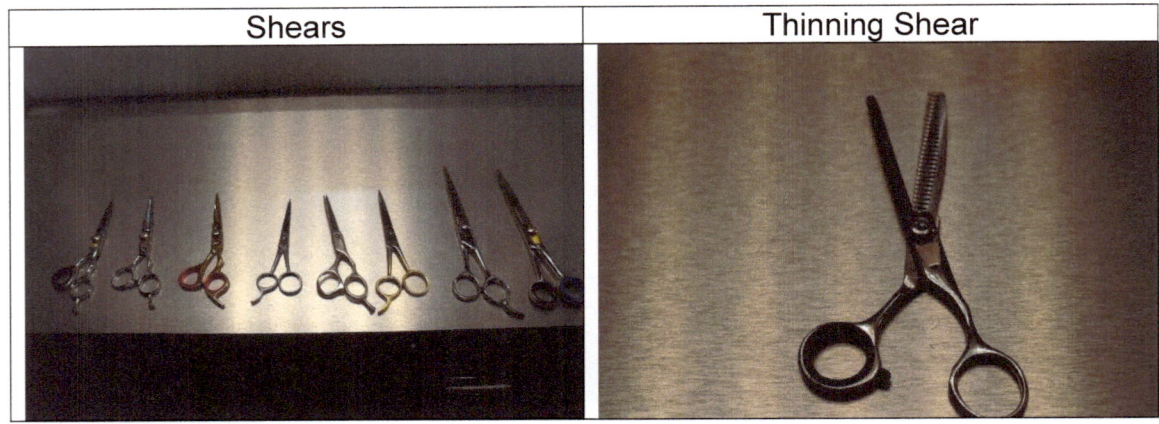	
Razor (Straight > Shaper > Safety)	Thinning Shear
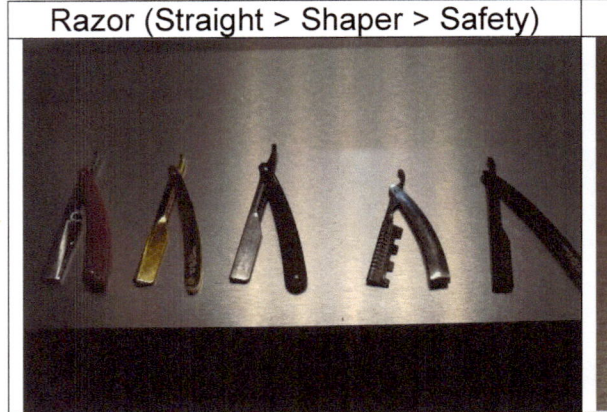	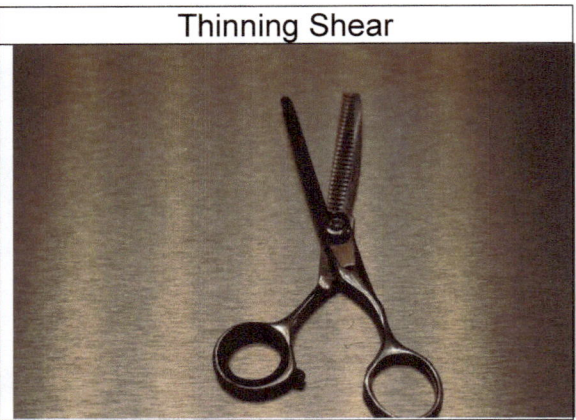
Comb	Picks
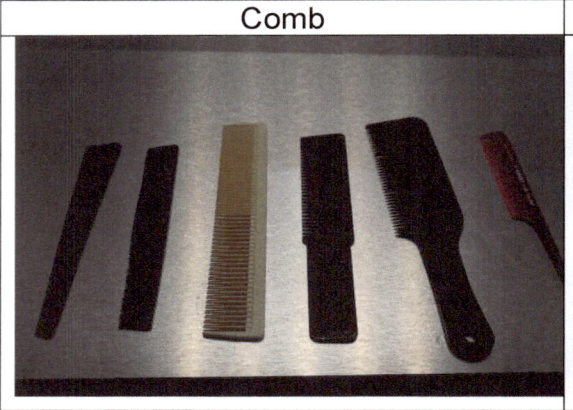	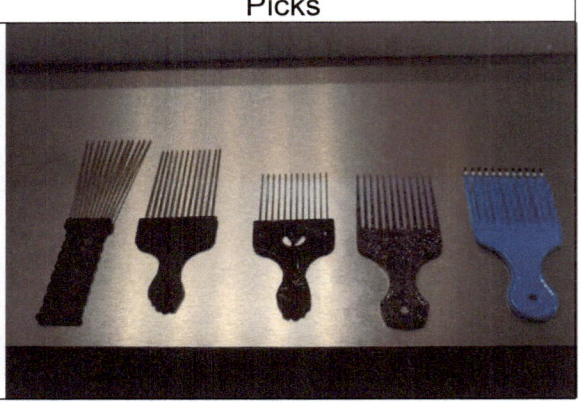

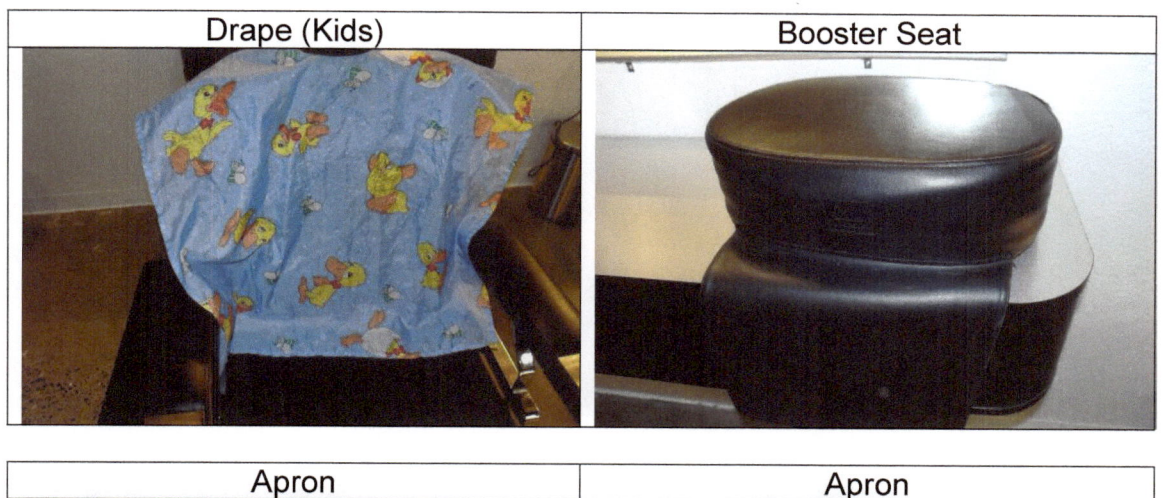
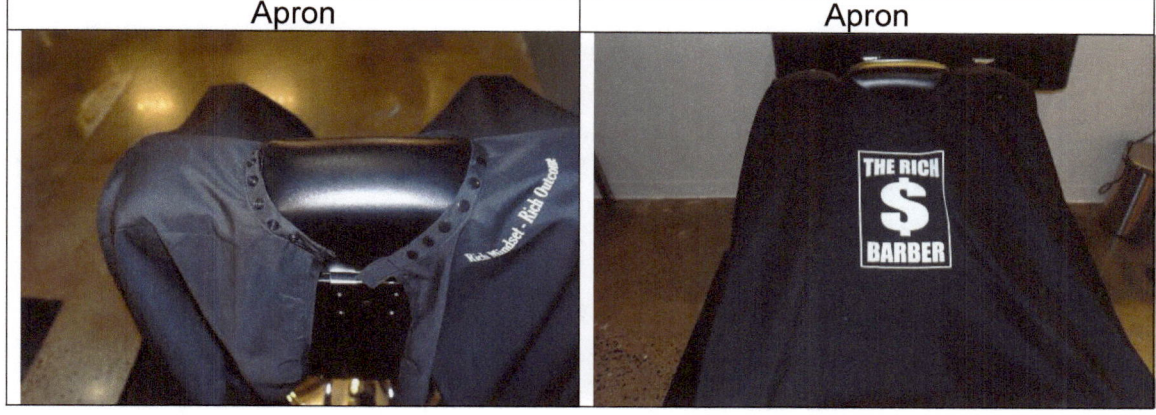

Supplies

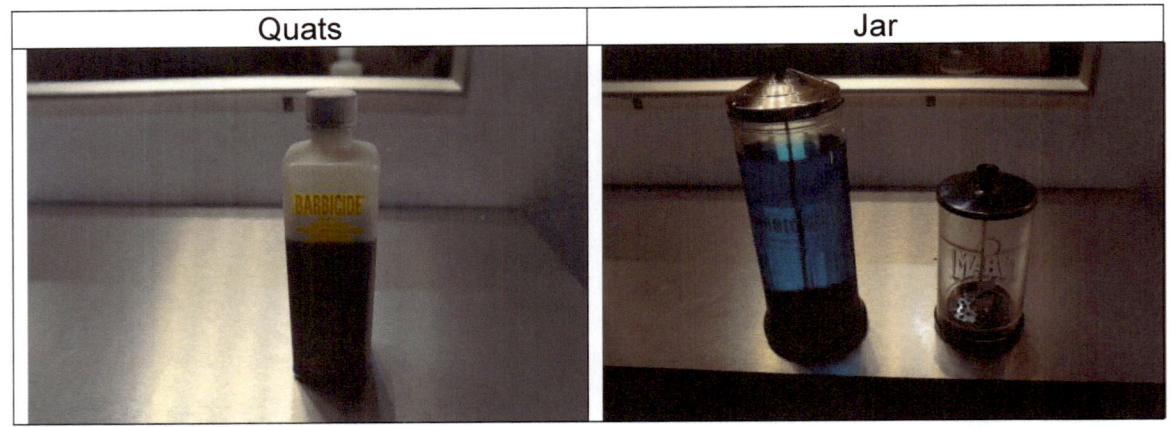

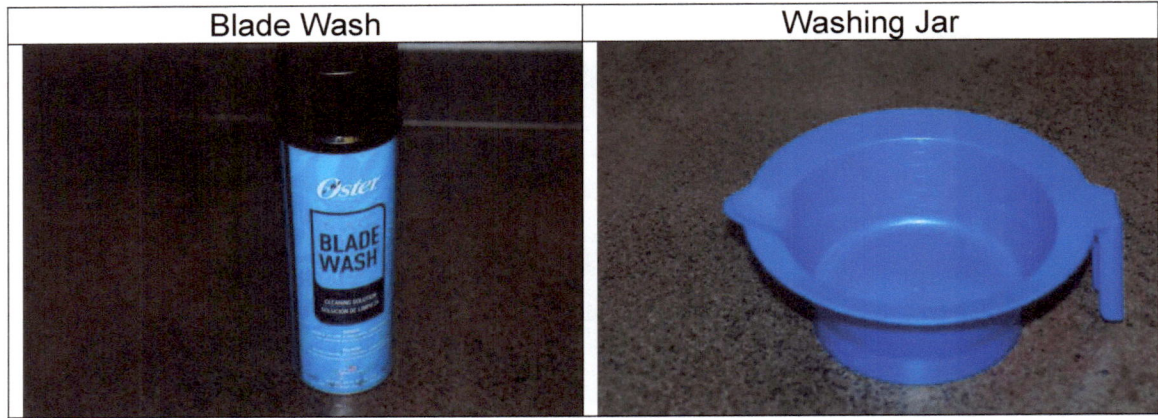

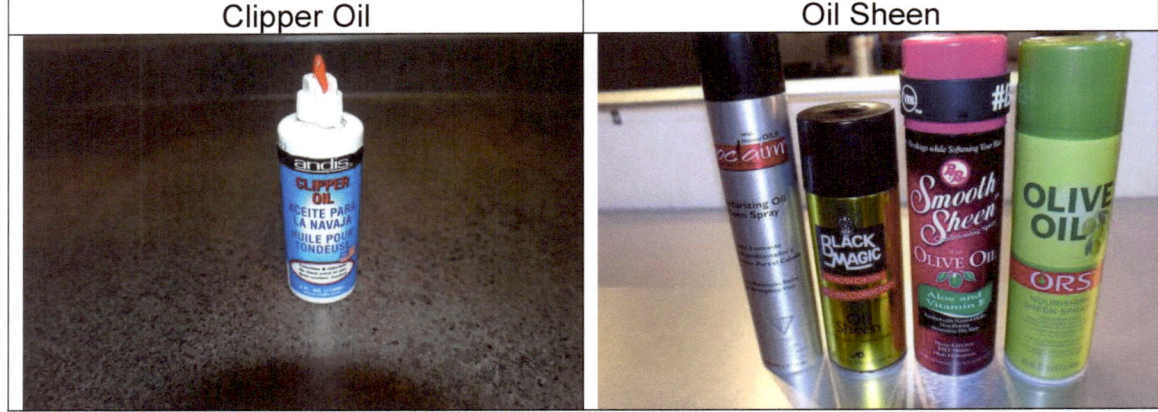

Pomade (Cream/Paste/Oil/Water)	Pomade
Pomade	Gel, Holding Gel
Astringent (Sea Breeze)	Astringent

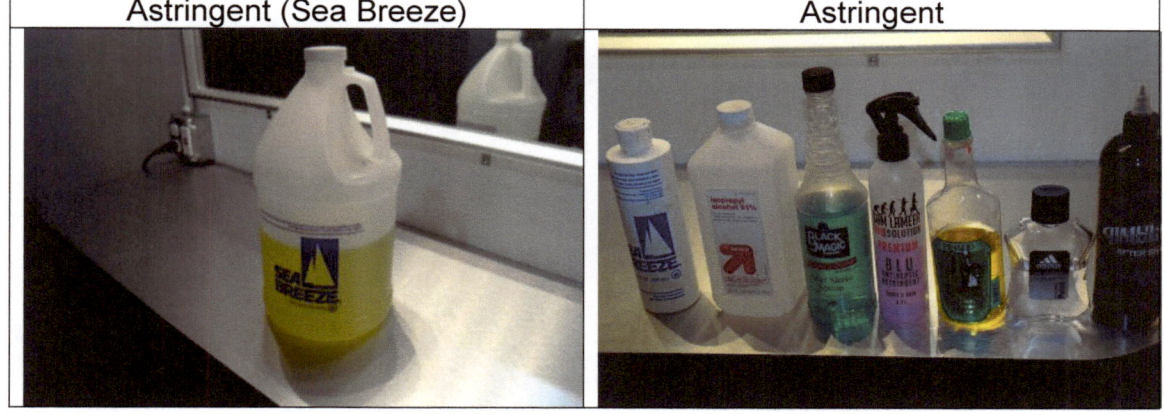

Power (Remove Hair)	Brush (Clean Clippers and Clients)
	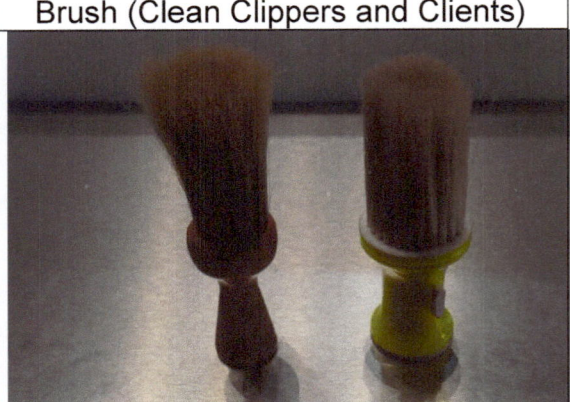
Neck Strips	Neck Strips
	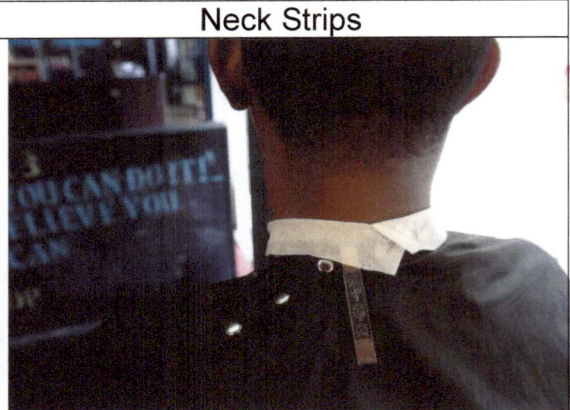

Record Keeping

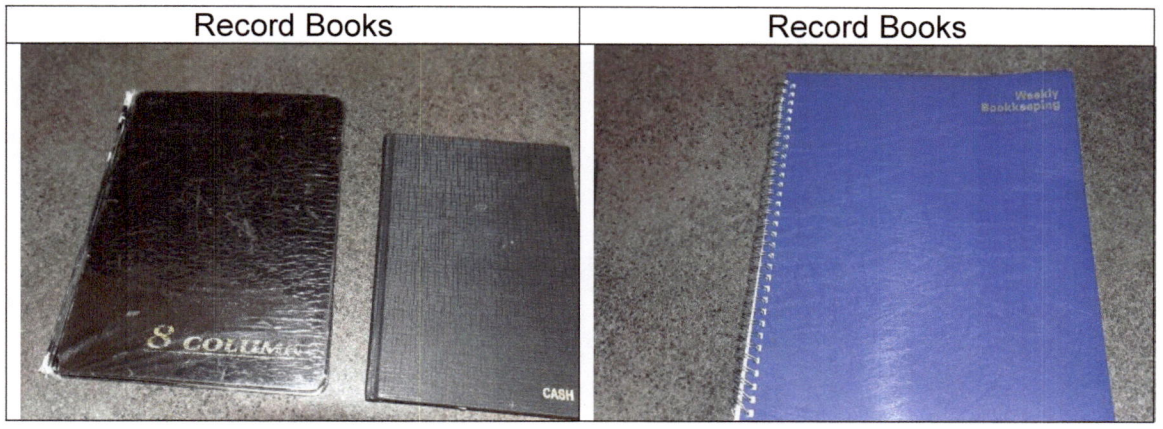

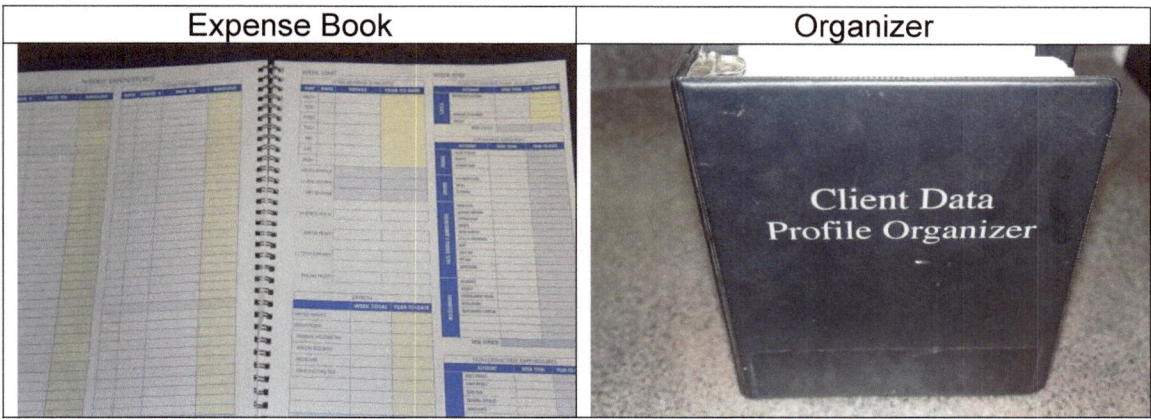

BARBER RECORD KEEPING BOOK

You may find a digital copy at
WWW.BETHEWORLDSGREATESTBARBER.COM/BARBERRECORDKEEPINGBOOK

Barber Record Keeping Sheet

Date	Paid To	CK# CASH	EDU/CON	DUES	ADS	SURPLUS	TRANS	GIFTS	MISC
January									
February									
March									
April									
May									
June									
July									
August									
September									
October									
November									

December

Date	Travel Method	Place	Person	Relation	Reason	Amount

AWAY-FROM-HOME TRAVEL EXPENSE (Not Counting Car Expenses)

DATE	Fare	P/T/B	Brfst	Lnch	Dinnr	Tips	Htel	Amt	Misc	Amt
Page Total										
Previous Total										
Accumulated Total										

Expense Sheet

EXPENSE	EXP LOG #1	EXP LOG #2	ENT LOG	AW. HOME LOG	TOTAL
BOOTH RENT					
PHONE					
ADS					
DUES					
EDU/CON					
SURPLUS					
TRANSACTIONS					
GIFTS					
EQUIP					
MEAL					
TRAVEL MLS					
TRAVEL LODGES					
AIRFARE					
GRAND TRANSACTIONS					

DATE	MILEAGE LOG	ODOMETER	MI SIN LAST	BUS	COMM	PERS	DEST
TOTAL MILES THIS PAGE							
ACCUMULATED TOTAL PREVIOUS PAGE							
ACCUMULATED TOTAL							

Travel Expense Sheet

Gas Money	Gallons	Odometer	MLS LST	MPG C/A

Parking & Tolls	Date	Cost	Non-Parking related Tolls and Commute Costs	Date	Cost	Grand Total

Maintenance Record

Date	Odometers	Oil/Lube	Wash	Repair	Cost

Automobile Annual Summary

Name	Purchase Date	Make	Date Business Use Began	Original Cost	Tax Basis

Automobile Annual Summary

Name	Reading at End of Year	Reading at Beginning Year	Total miles travelled in the year	Total Business miles from logs

Automobile Annual Summary

Name	Business Use	Auto Expenses	Gas Purchases	Parking & Tolls	Maintenance Cost	Insurance	License

Miscellaneous Income Source

Date	Source	Amount

Service Sales

Date	Source	Amount

Income

Date	Source	Amount

CUSTOMERS

"Do On To Others, As You Would Have Them Do On To You"

Managing Your Business

Customer service

You are entering a field that involves having very close and intimate interaction with individuals. You are responsible for the most important grooming to a man, which is his hair. Hair is the first thing most people see and notice about a person. It is always a privilege when someone trusts you with the responsibility of making them look great.

To provide great customer services, you will have to be as consistent as possible showing how you care about your responsibility, that you are listening and willing to follow directions, and you are creative enough to add your own contributions. Customer services is all about fulfilling your clients' emotional needs of being valued.

Must have to provide great customer service:

Patience: Be patient when client get frustrated or come in confused.

Attentiveness: Listen to what they are saying, both verbally and body language.

Communication Skills: Keep it simple no need to get to technical.

Knowledge of the style or product: Thorough knowledge of styles and products is critical to helping clients with their needs.

Ability to use positive language: Avoid using the word 'No'. If a client comes in when you are totally booked, schedule them at the closest time possible instead of saying No to servicing them.

Acting Skills: Every great Barber who provides customer service will need basic acting skills. It is necessary to maintain the usual cheery and upbeat persona in spite of dealing with people who are rude, unpleasant and grumpy.

Keeping your emotions under control: Leave behind your personal life whenever you step into the store.

Time management skills: Provide customer their required service in an efficient manner. If talking with a customer, be sure to keep cutting during the conversation. Ask questions that require more than a yes or no answer. Always try to entertain your client while you work efficiently.

Know your ability: Do not waste time trying to go above and beyond for a customer in an area where you will just end up wasting both of your time.

Ability to "read" a customer: Look and listen for subtle cues about their mood, patience level, personality, uncomfortable movements and you will go far in keeping your customer interaction positive.

A calming presence: Do not lose your cool. If someone else is grumpy; be calm, confident, and reassuring and you will be able to pacify even the most irate clients and turn them into lifelong customers.

Be goal-oriented: Have goals for time, greetings, and other things that build your business.

Ability to handle surprises: A barber can make a mistake and instantly tell the client that he made a mistake while cutting. A great barber will make the same mistake and stay calm, do whatever necessary to fix it as though it never happened.

There will be times where you may be confused on how to approach a challenging haircut. Respectfully enlist the help of a veteran barber who can give insight on how to approach the situation.

Persuasion skills: It is not about making a sales pitch, but rather about not letting potential clients slip away. You must create a compelling message that your service is worth purchasing or waiting for. You will have to have confidence in yourself, your service, your price for others to have confidence in you.

Tenacity: Put forth extra effort, do not cheat yourself or the customer by giving lazy service.

Closing ability: End the cut with confirmed *satisfaction*. Show that you care about getting it right, and that you are willing to keep going until you get it right. Even let your client determine what "right" is.

Willingness to learn: Those who do not seek to improve, they will be left behind by others more willing. Learn everything from better haircuts to business marketing. Watch veterans you admire, study and ask questions when appropriate. Watch videos, attend workshops, take photos so you can review and critique your work. Learning resources can be found at
www.betheworldsgreatestbarber.com/resources

Invest in your tools: Acquire the best tools and products. Keep replacing tools like old brushes, aprons, and drapes. Keep a good stock of astringent razors, neck strips etc. Products and tools can be found at
www.betheworldsgreatestbarber.com/productsandtools

Be confident: Have a firm and energetic handshake, the more excited you are to see people the more welcome, important, and comfortable they will feel.

Personal appearance: Barbers should present themselves as ready to work. Their apparel should stand out from clients in the shop. Wear clean and pressed clothes, maintain good personal grooming, have short and clean nails.

Language: Appropriate and clean language should be used in the shop. Some clients will use foul language without realizing the inappropriateness. Respectfully let them know to filter the language.

Ban sensitive conversations: Religion and politics are both high sensitive subjects. They can cause heavy influence on emotions and thus should be kept out of the shop.

Note: that barbershop arguments or debates can be very funny, informational, silly, offensive, and redundant. Know that most people feel that their stance or belief is the soundest idea in the room. Trying to change someone's mind by arguing their point and exposing hole in their arguments only makes them want to take a stronger stance and create a tense atmosphere.

Avoid distractions: They only slow you down. People walking by the window, television shows, conversations with other barbers, phone calls, emails etc. can all be distractions that slow down your cutting business. Always keep your hands moving.

Cleanliness: Wash your hands after every cut and sanitize your equipment.

Going Beyond Client Expectations

Be punctual: Be ready before your appointments. Inform clients if you are running late, offer them a beverage if you run late beyond five minutes.

Be respectful: "yes sir" "no sir" eye contact, firm hand shake, please, and thank you.

Be a good listener: Give confirmation that you understand. Do not interrupt, ask for clarification on things you do not understand.

Follow instructions: Wishes of the client is always more important. Demonstrate that you are able to give them exactly what they want. If you desire to do something different, share your vision without pressuring them into a style they do not want.

Just do your best: Have all your concentration on the task at hand. Focus only on making your client happy.

Exceeding Expectations

Be Knowledgeable: Acquire knowledge about hair care and products can recommend to your clients. They will take your recommendations because you are their trusted expert. Encourage clients to bring you questions about hair related topics.

Be Patient: Some people have social anxiety, insecurities, and confusion about their appearance. Have patience and gradually build trust and communication.

Attention to details: Focus on trimming commonly over looked like face sections; ear hair, eye brow hair, nose hair, neck hair. Ask for client's permission beforehand, you never know what they are comfortable with.

With long standing clients, it is often easy to assume what sort of service they require because you have gone through them so many times. No, never assume that client will keep wanting the same service, always confirm what sort of service they require.

Also at times, some clients will need specific sections of their head hair to grow, while other sections will need to be cut down. You are the professional here, know your craft and keep your client informed about what you are doing.

Keep a lint roller: Pick up hair from clients' clothes.

Stock up on Mints: Bad mouth odor should always be avoided. Try mint gums, also offer some to your clients.

Remember Names: Refer clients by their names. If you have trouble remembering, try writing down their names or associate them with their own personal goals they share with you.

Be Consistent: Maintain consistency in your service. Give all clients the same level of service and care.

Go beyond: After every cut, ask your client for any other service they desire.

Remember Life Events: Try to acquire one significant piece of information from your clients at every appointment.

Name	Telephone #	Email Address	Hair Style	Birthday

Appreciate referrals: Be thankful immediately.

Be Encouraging: Lift the spirits of all those around you.

Gift: Try doing the unexpected; give your client cards and small gifts that can touch their happy core.

Example Conversation

A) Hello sir. My name is X and yours?
B) My Name is X.

A) Well Mr. X, how can I make you look your best?
B) I want 1 on the side and 2 on the top.

A) 1 side, 2 top. No problem. Since this is my first time cutting your hair, I want to make sure we are on the same page, on the sides do you want skin showing or just a little bit of hair?
B) I want to see some skin by the temple, but have enough hair to have a line behind the ears.

A) That is great. Now two on the cop is going to take a lot off. Let me ask you, how long ago did you receive your last cut?
B) About a month ago.

A) OK, Great. (At this point always grab a guard that is one to two levels above what they mentioned. Cut a small area and allow them to see it in the mirror) since this is my first time cutting you and I know different barbers use different numbers, this portion I cut is a 3. I can continue using this if you like or we can use the two like you had stated. I like being on the safe side, because after its been cut I can't put the hair back on.
B) Thank you, I appreciate you taking the time. I would like a 2.

A) Great Mr. X. 2 it is; I appreciate your patience.

Routine of Service

This should be standard protocol. Always following it in order.

1. Cut

2. Clean
3. Style
4. Present Mirror

Remember that your goal is to make clients feel special towards themselves.

A) Is there anything else I can do?
B) No that will be it

A) I appreciate your patience once again and thank you for giving me the opportunity to cut your hair.
B) Oh your welcome, I'll definitely be coming back

A) Well allow me to give you a few business cards, one for you and two if any friends or family need a good barber.
B) Definitely.

A) I would also like to add you to my email list. I send out valuable information about my schedule, promotions, and hair care tips.
B) Great.

A) While I have you here, would you like to schedule your next appointment?
B) Yeah. How about 2 weeks from now, same time?

A) That's great. I'll see you then, Thanks again Mr. X, see you soon.

Other Good Practices

Do not talk over clients

Holding all out conversation with anyone but your client can be inappropriate and distracting to the person who just wants to relax and feel that you are focused on them.

Remember your hello

Enthusiastically say hello to everyone, and thank them for coming when they leave.

Get feedback

Ask clients how did the last cut workout for them? Find out what they liked and areas that you can improve on.

Know your clients

If you know they are in a relationship, ask how their *significant* other liked the cut. Doing this allows the client to freely express thoughts about your haircuts that they did not feel comfortable saying directly.

Clients know the best for themselves

Fight the urge to cut hair the way you want. As artists, we create styles for people to take on and feel amazing about themselves. There will be times that you will be asked to do a cut or style that you feel would look better your way. Talk with your client about what you feel, and offer various possibilities that you can envision, try finding some compromise between you and the clients vision.

Be vigilant of any signs of rejection; but know if the client rejects your recommendation; Do the service as requested. Consider this cut the beginning of long-term client/barber relationship, and as trust builds up, you can try changing the client's mind once you have established good and understanding communication.

For some reason, if you are strongly against cutting a requested style, then politely explain that you will not be able to fulfill their requests. Recommend another barber that can.

Understand that your work is challenging

Peoples' image revolves around hair so naturally you will have some clients that have many issues about their hair. You are the hair professional and they expect solutions from you. Make sure you come true to their expectations and deliver great service.

Never extend credit to deadbeats

This is a business and people will try to take advantage of you by asking you for discounted services, or a free cut for trying you out, or the *"I don't have a way to pay you now but later I will."* This is not good business! Don't do it! Now long standing clients there are exceptions you make on rare occasions that you have your clients back if you can but never for someone new! Don't prostitute your skills for less than your worth ever. Use best judgment when applying this principle.

Speed demons

You will also sometimes have clients who are always looking at their watch, asking you what time it is and how long will it take for the cut to finish.

Politely give a general time for your services and request a few extra minutes for errors. Before starting service, if client pressures you to finish within a certain, impossible time frame, politely suggest that they come back when they have more time.

Time consumers

The complete opposite of Speed Demons. These clients never want to leave, they will stare at their head for minutes, trying to find the slightest imperfection. Certain things are understandable if you did make an error, but those who just want extra attention or an ego boost are too time consuming and needy, it is generally better to let them go.

Remember, you do not want to spend fifteen minutes cutting and the next two hours fixing trivial details.

Focus on the elderly

Old men are great; they do not get cut often because they do not have much hair anyway. When they do get cut, they normally get in and out of your chair within 10-15 minutes and you get paid the same amount as you would for a 45-minute cut.

Focus on parents and children

Parents are great clients. They are very appreciative to have a nice place to take their little ones. Especially if you know a parent is coming in, try to make sure music and conversation is respectable.

Wearing cologne

Cologne are great in making you smell attractive and great, but you do not want to use too much cologne as certain scents may be offensive to some clients.

Help elderly and children with the chair

Make sure you provide adequate hand support to both elderly and children so they do not hurt themselves while getting on, or leaving the chair.

Sleepers

You will also get clients who feel comfortable and trusting enough to fall asleep. Try not to spin these clients around in the chair too fast, sometimes momentum will carry them right out of the chair.

Be careful when lining a sleeper. Head nods always seem to come at the wrong time, rest index finger on their forehead, that way you can control their movement.

Proper chair etiquette

Avoid straddling client or standing directly in front of them. Ask them to turn their head to you for easy cutting angles.

Always observe before combing

Before starting a cut comb through the hair, Identify swirls where hair changes direction. Observe different colors, texture, and density of hair. Check for any sore areas or moles bumps.

Careful with the razor

Avoid using razor on areas that show signs of existing bumps and irritation.

Present a mirror

Always give clients a clean mirror to look at themselves.

Understand guards

When working on a new client, many times they will tell you what guards to use without having full understanding of what they are talking about. Start with your largest guards and cut a small area, then show the client the length. "It's always easier to take more hair off than to put it back on."

Cleaning clients

After service, once the client is standing, always dust off their shoulders.

Keep hair from gathering up on clients face by dusting them off regularly. Hair is very sharp and can easily get into eyes. Have your off-hand on client's forehead, this keeps cut hair away from their face.

Meet the waves

Over time you will notice very high and very moderate volume of clients entering your shop. Ride the wave, if the beginning of the week is light, it is more than likely that the weekend will be very busy. If rain keeps people away for a few days. Know, that once the weather turns back to nice your clients will be calling to set an appointment. Certain times of year you will be busier, especially around school and holiday schedules.

The Art of listening

Listening is essential to your success. Why? Because listening effectively will tell you almost everything you need to know about a person. Everyone will give you verbal clues on their dislikes and likes. Paying attention to the client's tone, voice, observing what they speak cheerfully and passionately about, allows you to build upon positive cues and talking points to engage in.

When building relationships, creating an experience where someone feels comfortable bearing their soul to you is key to the longevity of your relationship. That relationship is very powerful in business because through strong relationships you gain clients and consumers of your services for life.

Become a Student of BODY LANGUAGE

The body often speaks louder than the tongue. Facial expressions communicate a lot, but it is not always the dominant expression that you see on a person's face that tells the true feelings of the person. What you need to understand is Micro Expressions.

Micro Expressions

A **micro expression** is a brief, involuntary facial expression shown on the face of humans according to emotions experienced. They usually occur in high-stakes situations, where people have something to lose or gain. Micro-expressions occur when a person is consciously trying to conceal all signs of how they are feeling, or when a person does not consciously know what they are feeling.

Becoming proficient in reading body language and verbal cues
Some people have a natural ability to read a person's emotion or the vibe that persons gives off. They can use these skills to engage in most pleasing conversations. Over time, you can gain enough data from your study of people that from very short brief interactions you can gather comprehensive information on the personality of people.

Connecting with Clients

1. Where did you hear about us?

2. How often do you like to get your hair cut?

3. When was your last haircut?

4. What did you like and dislike about your last cut?

5. If a phone call comes in, ask them if they mind if you answer?

6. Thank them for their patience, if it is going to take time to cut their desired style, then ask them for further patience.

7. Ask about kids, family, sport teams, favorite cities, job.

8. Pick a few talking points to remember for the next time you see them.

9. Ask them to schedule their next appointment.

10. Send confirmation email or text them as a reminder.

11. If clients cancel with/without calling, always show concern about their welling being first and foremost. Then encourage future behavior for contacting you in case of cancellation.

12. If a client share an accomplishment with you, make sure you congratulate them.

13. Develop ways to show additional appreciation. This can be kind words, a personal note, small gift certificate, discounted haircut, gift, or hosing a client party.

14. Never expect that you are going to get tips. Some clients will never tip you, so do not bank on the possibility of that tip coming. People tip you by choosing you to cut their hair and sharing their life experience with you. If you are not satisfied with what you receive, then raise your service price so you do not short change yourself.

15. Make sure you get paid for your time and service, which can be hard at times because of the relationship factor in this business. Remember this is a business and there is nothing wrong in getting fully compensated for your services.

16. When draping, do not go over the clients head with drape or strips.

17. Do not blow air on the clippers.

18. Do not flap drapes near clients.

19. Enclose hair from corner to corner, flip so hair can fall and pop twice

20. Before applying astringent, alert the client to the possibility of stinging.

Customer Expect

1. **Speedy response**: If you communicate via text, voice mail, email, make sure that when a customer reaches out to you, that you return their call within 24 hours. Having an online booking system eliminates a good 95% of client calls and allows clients to book appointments online.

   Voice mail message should provide your name and inform people the times you are accepting calls, when you will be returning calls (either at certain times or within 24 hours). Direct them to your online booking system or have them text you if responding to text messages are more convenient for them. You can also set a permanent message at the footer of your email that describes your hours of operations, how you will be returning emails and link to web site to handle booking.

2. **Customer expect accuracy:** Keeping appointment times, performing required haircuts, understanding all requirements before the cut starts.

3. **Consistent service:** This means that the general experience should be the same every time the client visits. Do not vary in how you perform your service. Changing the client experience creates uncertainty and degrades their freedom to choose the service experience they are purchasing.

4. **Customers expect punctuality:** Customers expect business to be running as displayed on their hours of operations. If shop hours are 9-5 there should be barber(s) on duty ready to work. Displaying a Welcome sign is an invitation to a potential customer, make sure that you have someone to greet the person and to schedule them for later if necessary.

5. **Expect the money back guarantee:** Almost every business and service offer clients a money back guarantee. For unsatisfied customers, just avoid the energy in arguing about your payment and the quality of your service.

   It is better to free yourself from the hassle and wasted energy on an unhappy or possibly unpleasant individual by just taking it as a learning experience. Show sincerity and genuine concern, express your desire to get better. Someone who likes you and is pleased with the quality of service you provide will overlook your mistake and give you a second or third chance.

6. **No hidden fees:** Customers do not want to be hit with hidden fees, make sure that pricing for services are displayed, and that inform the customers beforehand about additional fees for using a credit card or check.

7. **Universal promotions:** Customers expect promotion and pricing to be

redeemable with every barber in the shop. If you are running a separate promotion or not participating in a promotion, make sure that such is expressed clearly in all the media sent out via text, email, flier, website, mobile, social media etc.

8. **Maintain communication:** If a customer makes complaints or leaves comments on your service on the social media, be sure to respond to it quickly.

9. **Be unique:** Clients dislike overly scripted greetings and responses. Practice your greeting and responses so they sound natural when you are communicating and marketing yourself to new clients. Practice your excitement and enthusiasm then you will own your words and the way they are received.

10. **Empower clients:** Expect customers to feel as if they are always right. Clients are empowered now with online ways to let the world know about the quality of your service, so try to treat customer like they are always right.

11. **Respect clients:** Your customer is a "Star" and it is your job to treat them like such, so give them star quality service. Customers pay you for your service, regardless if they make millions or pennies. At the end of your service they are handing their money over to you.

12. **Remember names:** In this business, there is no faster and more reliable way to build a rapport, cultivate likeness, and make a great lasting impression than to remember a client's name. In turn, not remembering someone's name make them feel of less value.

The Art of Handling People

As a barber you will be constantly dealing with new people whom have new personalities and new issues. In this chapter you will learn how to win more friends and build great foundations for life long relationships

Objective: To show you what and what not to do when dealing with people.

Barbering is very much so the art of human relations. If you embody the principles laid out in this chapter no matter where you go or environment you choose to run your business, you will be able to have much success and grow your client base.

Principle 1:

Don't criticize, condemn or complain.

The only way to get anyone to either sit in your chair or give you their money or time is to make them want to give it to you. And you do so by not judging them, or making fun of them. And definitely don't repel them by talking about all your problems.

So how do you get a walk-in that is sitting in your chair for the first time or someone you just met to want to give you a chance to be their barber?
They have to like you. You have to make an impression in a very short time that will make someone actually want to show you some support and try your services.

The Secret: When meeting someone new let the conversation focus be entirely about them. Make eye contact, Display attentiveness with your body language. Be enthusiastic interested in the other person and they will be interested in you and like the attention you've shown them. See chapter Law of Retaliation which goes into more detail of why this is so successful.

What most people want

1. Health and the preservation of life.
2. Food.
3. Sleep.
4. Money and the things money will buy.
5. Life in the hereafter
6. Sexual gratification
7. The well-being of our children.
8. A feeling of importance.

Everybody likes a compliment and deep down inside wants to be appreciated and important. Passing on the opportunity to let someone have it.
Avoid flattery, as people can see through your B.S and will feel your trying to butter them up or run some type of mental game. Be honest and genuine in your appreciation of others.

* Remember that a person's name is to that person the sweetest and most important sound in any language.

* Be a good listener. Encourage others to talk about themselves. Once you find what someone is most passionate about, focus your conversation around that.

* Ask yourself "What is there about him/her that I can honestly admire?"

* **Golden rule**

* **Make the other person feel important and do it sincerely.**

The following pages are some amazing principals from the book "How To Win Friends And Influence People" I highly recommend it to all Barbers,

SIX WAYS TO MAKE PEOPLE LIKE YOU

Principle 1

Become genuinely interested in other people.

Principle 2

Smile.

Principle 3

Remember that a person's name is to that person the sweetest and most important sound in any language.

Principle 4

Be a good listener. Encourage others to talk about themselves.

Principle 5

Talk in terms of the other person's interest

Principle 6

Make the other person feel important, and be sincere.

WIN PEOPLE TO YOUR WAY OF THINKING

Principle 1

The only way to get the best of an argument is to avoid it altogether.

Principle 2

Show respect for the other person's opinions. Never say, "You're wrong."

Principle 3

If you are wrong, admit it quickly and emphatically.

Principle 4

Begin in a friendly way.

Principle 5

Get the other person saying "yes" immediately.

Principle 6

Let the other person do a great deal of the talking.

Principle 7

Let the other person feel that the idea is his or hers.

Principle 8

Try honestly to see things from the other person's point of view.

Principle 9

Be sympathetic with the other person's ideas and desires.

Principle 10

Appeal to the nobler motives.

Principle 11

Dramatize your ideas.

Principle 12

Throw down a challenge

BE A LEADER

A Leader's job often includes changing your people's attitudes and behavior. Some suggestions to accomplish this:

Principle 1

Begin with praise and honest appreciation

Principle 2

Call attention to people's mistakes indirectly.

Principle 3

Talk about your own mistakes before criticizing the other person.

Principle 4

Ask questions instead of giving direct orders.

Principle 5

Let the other person save face.

Principle 6

Praise the slightest improvement and praise every improvement. Be "hearty in your approbation and lavish in your praise."

Principle 7

Give the other person a fine reputation to live up to. Create a reputation of a good leader that others aspire to have.

Principle 8

Use encouragement. Make a fault or a mistake seem easy to correct.

Principle 9

Make the other person happy about doing the thing you suggest.

Ways to Making more Money in Your Barbershop.

1. **Selling Products:** People are always looking for the best hair products to keep up their appearance. You are their trusted authority and your recommendation is very influential. Sell products you like and can educate your clients confidently about.

2. **Vending Machines:** Great way to offer snacks and cold drinks to clients.

3. **Tournaments:** Host a game tournament of some sort. Charge for entry, which will go towards the Grand prize, and keep the rest for profits. Provide food and drinks for sale, and take complimentary pictures.

4. **Have Various:** Levels of Service: Have low end, basic, and high end services to offer.

Service Value Pyramid

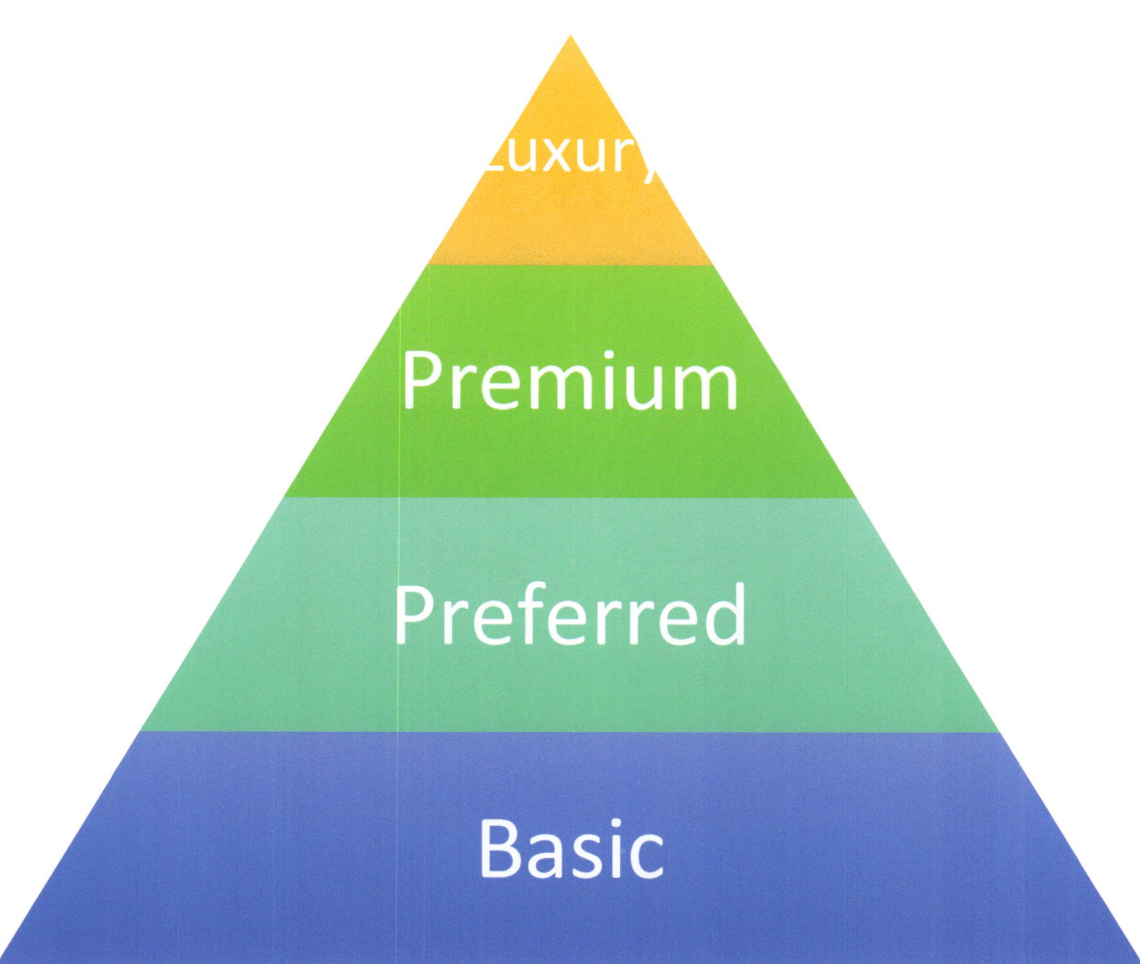

IN CASE OF EMERGENCIES CALL 911

THERE MIGHT BE A TIME WHEN YOU HAVE A CLIENT IN THE CHAIR THAT MAY SUFFER FROM A MEDICAL EMERGENCY. PROVIDED ARE A FEW GUIDES TO FIRST AID

I have all the links to printable material on my website: www.betheworldsgreatestbarber.com

Fig:1-2 source: www.algra.com/first-aid-posters Fig:3 source: http://safety-signs.comompliancesigns.com

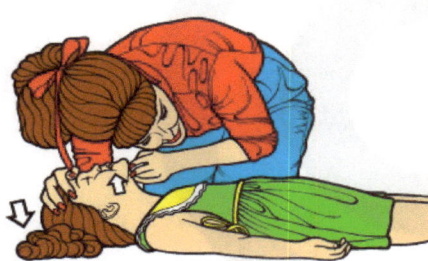
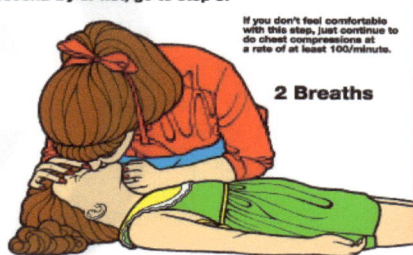
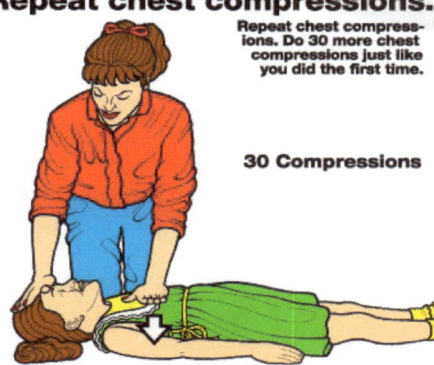
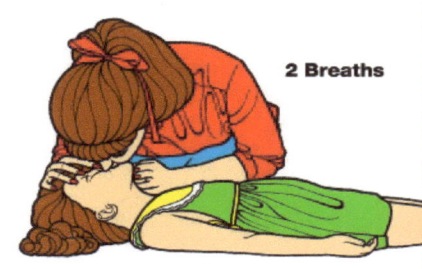

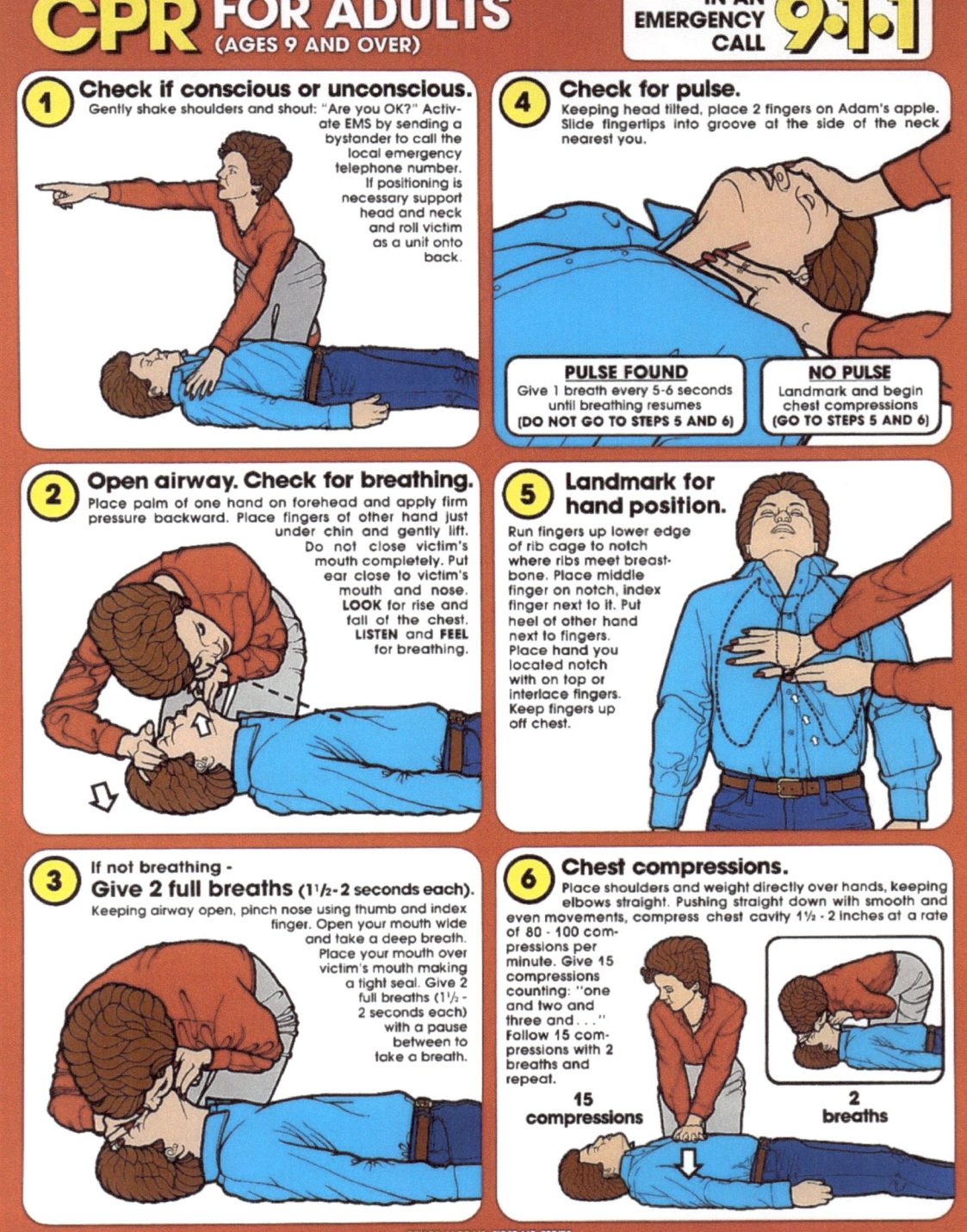

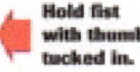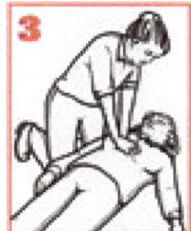

MARKETING

"You Must First Be A Consistent Barber For You To Have A Consistent Clientele"

Marketing

In this business, marketing is everything. There are two categories in which to market and when employed with consistency will yield great results. The reason you need to continuously market is so clientele can continue to grow, to build a continuous stream of clients who can support you.

Every year changes in life will have clients moving on whether for school or job, relationship or death, clients will come and go.

Un-focused Approach – what not to do.

Bounces from action to action, never becoming consistent with any set of habits. Whatever way you market yourself, you have to be consistent. You have to be focused, fearless; you have to make contact with others, and also you have to be consistent yourself for your clients to be consistent.

Include every client into your marketing efforts. From day one, when you get a chance to pass them a card give them a few. "One to use, and two to pass along to friends and family."

Maintain Regular Contact

Keep at least monthly clients with all your regular clients. Track and remind them how long it has been since their last cut and invite them to stop by your shop.

An Item of value

It can be something as simple as information about a shampoo that you found to be good. If you are an amazon affiliate, you can copy and paste the link into your emails and if the clients purchase, you will receive a percentage of the sale. See amazon affiliate program for more information.

It can also be a calendar of your upcoming days of or a holiday reminder. Either through email or text, your clients should be hearing from you on major holidays.

Referrals

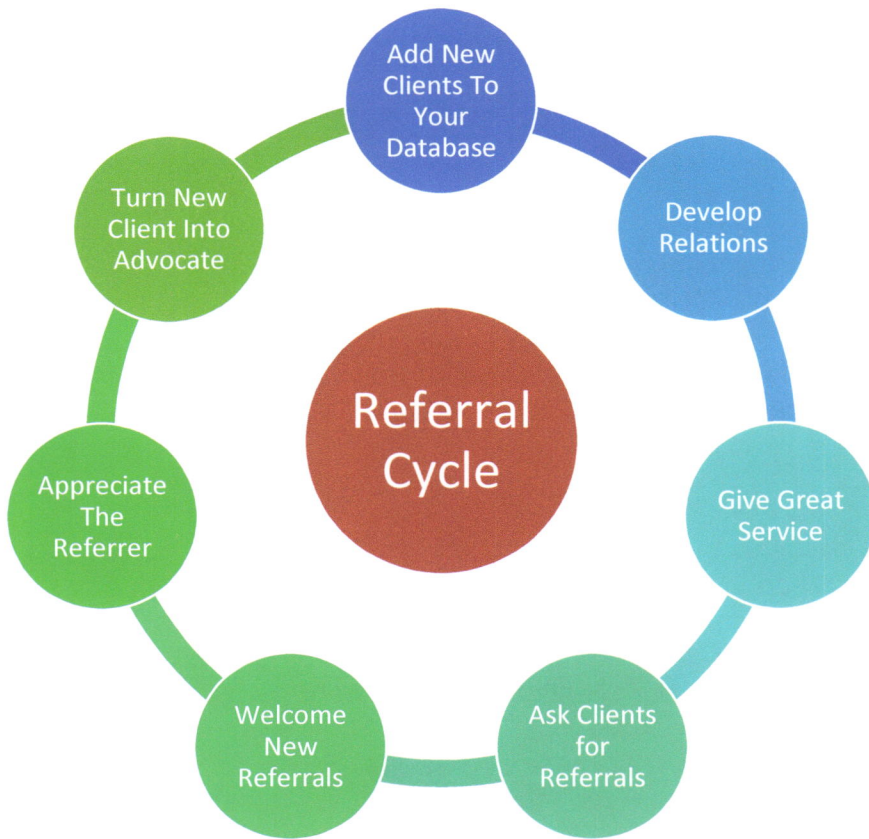

Understanding Types of Clients

All clients are important, but to be effective in your efforts and actions, you should focus on the group of people who yield the best returns in terms of referral with the most attention.

Make a list dividing your current clientele and contacts into four categories, include family and friends.

'A' Clients are those who have referred business to you already.
'B' Clients are those if asked, they would refer.
'C' Clients are repeat clients but have not referred business.
'D' Clients are those who you need to delete from your database.

Focus first on clients who already know and like you and would love to hear from you. Call them have a little small talk and use the "oh by the way if you or any friends or family that may need a great barber I am never too busy for you or any of your referral."

A great question to ask to stimulate conversation and learn from is by asking people "if someone was to ask you if you could refer a good barber would I be the person you recommend?" but only ask this to people whom you are close with or have a good standing relationship.

After you talk to them write them a personal note. Tell them that "It was great talking with you", thanking them for their referrals.

These are also the clients that if you get a chance to be a patron, go visit them at their business.

Appreciating

You should never offer rewards or bonuses for referring clients to you. Instead you should offer them your greatest appreciation and thanks. The referring process should always be considered a fun activity.

Appreciating should never be limited to just thanking referrals, take your time to pass out notes to all returning regular clients and newer clients. A great way to show true appreciation to your clients is to write them personal notes. Hand-written personal notes are always better than computer-printed notes, even if you wrote them both yourself.

This is because hand-written notes instantly show that you took time – a barber's most important commodity – to show them your appreciations, it shows that you really mean it!

If you pass out computer-printed appreciation notes, it may not ensure that they actually even be read because people may think of it as 'generic printed jargon', whereas everyone will certainly read a hand-written note.

When to Appreciate

Obviously, the thank you notes you write will need to have a purpose to be thankful for. Below is a list for occasions that may warrant a personal note.

- When a client stops by your shop for a cut
- When a client refers someone to your shop
- When a new client returns the second time
- When a client returns before your expectation
- When a client schedules their next appointment with you

- When a client makes payment for a service

Example Notes

"Dear John,
Thank you for referring your brother Eric to my shop. I can assure you that they will receive great service from me. I highly appreciate your referral.
Have a great day,
Alex"

"Dear Bill,
It was a great opportunity to service your hair today. I look forward to working on you again and expanding our relationship.
Best of Luck,
Joey"

Popping By

Consider popping by your client's workplaces sometimes. Doing so helps expands your relation with your client and make them much more likely to return for their next cut.

Ideally, you should have a small gift or token to present to your clients, nothing too special just something that shows them your appreciation. A pop-by shows your clients that you are willing to spend your own time to make sure they keep returning to you.

Dedicate one day for visiting, starting with your most favorite and regular clients and working downwards. Try to keep the meetings short and sweet and represent the great quality of your shop by being confident and enthusiastic. You could also be considering visiting on special days or holidays, plan these visits so you have the highest chance for having that client come for a cut, maybe visit a week before these special days.

- Hanukkah
- Christmas
- Mother's/Father's Day
- Independence Day
- Back-To-School
- Your own client party

Developing a Center of Influence

Use the following list to "jog" your memory for additional names of contacts. Ask yourself if you know anyone who is at all involved in any of the following. Write name next to each.

Accountant
Advertising
Aerobics
Airline
Alarm Systems
Animal Health/Vet
Apartments
Appraisers
Architects
Art
Athletics
Attorney
Automobile
Baby-sitters
Banking
Barber
Bartender
Baseball
Beauty Salon
Beeper
Bible School
Boats
Bonds/Stocks
Bookkeeping
Bowling
Brokers
Builders
Cable TV
Camping
Carpet Cleaning
Cellular Phones
CPA's
Chiropractors
Church
Cleaners
Colleges
Computer
Construction
Consulting

Contractors
Cosmetics
Country Clubs
Credit Union
Day Care
Delivery
Dentists
Dermatologists
Doctors
Dry Wall
Electrician
Engineering
Firemen
Fishermen
Florist
Furniture
Gardens
Golfing
Groceries
Gymnastics
Hair Care
Handicapped
Handyman
Hardware
Health Club
Health Ins.
Horses
Hospitals
Hotels
Hunting
Insurance
Investments
Jewelry
Laundries
Lawn Care
Libraries
Limousines
Loans
Management
Manufacturing
Mechanics
Medical
Mortgages
Motels
Museums
Music

Mutual Funds
Newspapers
Nurses
Nutrition
Office Machines
Office Furniture
Optometrists
Orthodontist
Pediatricians
Pedicures
Pensions
Pest Control
Pets
Pharmacies
Phones
Physician
Plumbing
Podiatrist
Pools
Preschools
Printing
Property Mtg.
Rental Agencies
Resorts
Restaurants
Roofing
Satellites
School
Secretaries
Shoe Repair
Siding
Signs
Skating
Skiing
Skydiving
Soccer
Softball
Software
Spas
Sporting Goods
Surgeons
Tailors
Teachers
Telecommunications
Tennis
Theaters

Title Comp.
Training
Typesetting
Universities
Video
Waste
Weddings
Wine

Community

Client Mini-gatherings

Business Meetings

Annual Client Parties

Annual Client Parties

Build your clientele internally by investing into those that like you already. Hosting client parties is a great way to achieve that.

Passing out Business Cards

You should ideally be passing out at least five business cards per day. Wherever you go, you should have a goal to meeting and passing along your contact information to at least one person.

If you have downtime in the shop, use that time for marketing. Go outside and meet someone, introduce yourself and make a connection, then pass out your card. Inside the shop, look as though you are ready to work. Always stand ready behind your chair whenever a client walks in.

Sign Holder

Go to Community Events

The chance to meet more people means opportunity to meet more potential clients.

The secret behind getting people interested in what you do is by first become interesting and enthusiastic about what they are doing. Wear your barber smock next time you are out people recognize the smock and will ask if you are a barber and where you cut at.

Also considering Investing in barber apparel. Hats, T-shirts etc.

Volunteer

There are usually events happening in your local community, in which you can communicate and help those who need help. Community events are fulfilling opportunities and great experiences to capture.

Use Social Media

Use social media to share your excitement and enthusiasm about your shop and events.

Share before-and-after photos of cuts. Share "words of encouragement," be someone that inspires others to be there best. Share some cool hair tips, or just update your regular clients on Facebook. You can even recommend good products to your clientele using Amazon affiliate links. For examples, go to my website:www.betheworldsgreatestbarber.com

Your shop should also have a good signage.

Tip: *Know that the barber, not the barbershop, determines the success of the barber. You can be just as successful cutting at home or at a shop.*

Use Fliers

Have a list of services to recommend and add them to it. This is called the Value Ladder.

The Ladder works like this; the start of the ladder is often referred to as bait to attract clients to you, this could be some service or amenity you provide for free. The goal is to make your bait so enticing that your fish wants to bite and sit your chair.

The end of the ladder is your primary service; this service has your set price associated to it. Ideally, you should think of unique and cheaper service to provide, and also some luxurious and expensive services too.

This way you can scale up your clients to different services after you have given them a valuable service and educated them on additional services you offer. Once you have identified the high-end spenders, you can develop additional services that keep moving them up the ladder.

For instance: It can be a shampoo service, or an expensive multi-week hair care conditioning service.

Create a website

1. Purchase your domain name

2. Choose a web host and sign up for an account

3. Design your web pages

4. Test your website

5. Implement a money making strategy or payment collection

6. Get your site noticed by introducing it to Google or Bing

Start a YouTube channel

Post videos of your work, tips and advice about hair.

1. Make sure you are signed into YouTube.

2. Go to all my channels.

3. If you want to make a YouTube channel for a Google+ page that you manage, you can choose it here. Otherwise, click "Create a New channel."

4. Fill out the details to create your new channel.

Consider

- Do you have the skills to create content? If not, there are many online assistants available.

- Does my story fit on the type of platform I choose to relay it in?

- Does my audience prefer specific kinds of contents?

- Share what you know with your clients, friends, and business partners. Do speaking engagements in person and online.

- Always present content that attract a lot of your potential clients. Know your pitch. It should not matter if you are face to face or online, be able to express what you do, why you do it, why it matters, and what is in it for them in about 30 seconds.

Law of Retaliation

Ask your clients to give you their business or job info, so you can refer services to them and help their business grow. Become a referral maker for others.

The key to get others interested in what you are doing is to be genuinely interested and enthusiastic about what they are doing. After you have poured all this attention or interest into someone else, The Law of Retaliation comes into effect.

The law is simple, what you give out to people, whether it be frown, compliment, or support, you will get it back sooner or later.

Own Your Niche

As barbers, we have a wide array of skills that we do daily. Pick one service you do exceptionally well and market that one service more than the rest. It will build awareness and separates you from the others.

- Offer social media promotion, coupon sales, exclusive offer.

- Register and promote your business with online accounts, yelp and yahoo local

- Send out press releases about your business

- Follow up with old clients

- Attend free events and conferences outside the hair industry. Look forward to meeting new people and bring business cards

- Brand your vehicle

- Give out promotion codes and samples of products

- Partner with other businesses

Become Part of your community

Some of your greatest fun will be the interaction with clients outside of the customer service provider role you normally play; barbecue at the park, fight night, video game tournaments, chess tournaments, dominoes tournaments, super bowl parties are some of the funniest events for you and your clients.

You will be surprised at how much people pull together to make an event special. Clients bring food alcohol and family to hang out with you and it's a great feeling. Remember to take lots of pictures email them to your guests.

Make laminates of the event photos as little keepsake for people, even include t-shirts. You can also charge an admission fee if you want the party to pay for itself. Raffles and games along with music will keep the energy up and the atmosphere fun for everyone.

This is also a great way to get people interacting, and since you know so many people on an intimate level, it is fun matching great people in your sphere together.

Community service

Many local churches or organization have events for the homeless, kids returning back to school, cancer fundraisers etc. Being able to give an hour or two of your time and skill is rewarding unto itself and it always gives future benefits.

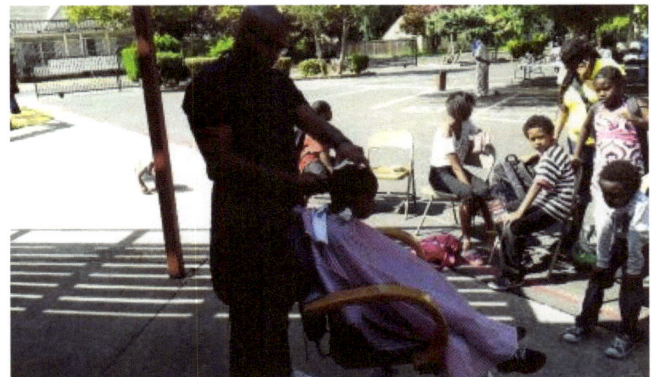
Back pack and haircuts for back to school event at local church

Dedicated Apparel

ACHIEVING GOALS

"If One Advances Confidently In The Direction Of Their Dreams, And Endeavors To Lead A Life Which They Have Imagined, They Will Meet With A Success Unexpected In Common Hours." Henry David Thoreau

To Achieve Your Dreams...Remember You're A, B, C's!

Avoid negative people, things and habits
Believe in your self
Consider things from every angle
Don't give up
Enjoy life today, yesterday is gone, and tomorrow may never come
Family and friends are hidden treasures. Seek them and value them.
Give more than you planned to give.
Hang on to your dreams.
Ignore those who try to discourage you.
Just do it!
Keep on trying, no matter how hard it seems, it will get better.
Love yourself first and foremost.
Make it happen.
Never lie, cheat, or steal. Always strike a fair deal.
Open your eyes and see things as they really are.
Practice makes perfect.
Quitters never win and winners never quit.
Read, study and learn about everything important in your life.
Stop procrastinating.
Take control of your own destiny.
Understand yourself in order to better understand others.
Visualize it.
Want it more than anything.
Xccelerate your efforts.
You are unique in all of creation; nothing and NO ONE can replace YOU!
Zero in on your target, and go for it!

By Wanda Hope Carter

Gaining Success

Achieving Top Productivity

Success only comes through great efficiency and productivity. In order to achieve success, you must be able to efficiently conduct the following: personal management, time management and energy management.

Personal Management

To achieve the highest productivity, you must know all your strengths and be able to use them to your advantage. Model your business strategy after whatever sort of cutting you do best, while taking on and overcoming tough challenges can feel great, but sometimes it is better to source the work to someone else if you feel you are not sufficiently experienced. That time can be better spent on clients you can easily tackle.

Acknowledge that it is your own responsibility to ensure that you are working for attaining the highest possible productivity. There is no point in taking in more work than you can safely chew, so do not overwork or overload yourself. Always track your working statistics and compare with the last day's numbers. Remember that you will only be getting busier as time passes and clients build up, so always have a long-term plan that ensures the highest efficiency and productivity of your service.

Time Management

Never spend too much time taking breaks, keep them moderate but long enough that work does not stress you out. Maintain a consistent time of approaching and leaving your shop, try to always be the first to enter and last to exit.
Never spend too long time on clients you know that you can never please. If there is a rush of clients in your shop, try to reach a good balance between speed and cut quality so you do not lose out on the impatient clients, otherwise take your time to mark the quality of your work and impress your customer!

Energy Management

In order to be successful at work, you must be motivated and energized, everyone reaches a point in their career when they sometimes do not feel motivated to work, even if they are very passionate about it. There are a number of things you can do to help keep up your motivation, such as having written short-term goals to accomplish, taking good care of your mind and body, and engaging with like-minded people.

If you are consistent with meeting your goals, tracking your progress of your set goals, having good accountability of your work, and work towards visual anchors, you are set on the path of gaining top productivity. Always keep in mind to give yourself sufficient break times so you do not overwork yourself.

There is nothing worse than experiencing some activity or conversation that saps your motivation of work. Stay far away from dramas and personal life issues during working time, stress can also play a huge factor in draining your motivation.

Ideally, you should have a set goal and a sense of direction of your work and there will be nothing to stop you from reaching your true and top potential.

Change What You Expect

No deep fulfilling success can come to you if you do not work for it. There is great power in your mind and your personal ability to determine the destination of your life. By choosing what you expect out of life will determine what life experiences you will have.

Be someone who views life as a blessing, that all of treasures of life are yours and that you can be and do anything you put your mind to. This powerful vibration sent out from your thoughts and beliefs will return to you with amazing achievements. Inspirations, ideas, solutions, and plans of action will enter your brain like magic, but you must become a person of action and implement what you have been given.

Symptoms of Barbers without Goals

1. Feel like they're in a rut
2. Frustrated by lack of growth
3. No purpose to their daily activities
4. Lack of motivation and energy

Set Goals For

- Saving
- New clients
- Business innovations
- Time efficiency
- Analysis and revision of cutting practices and habits to increase quality

and efficiency
- Tracking Business Activity
- Maintaining communication with old clients

Keys to Goal

- Specific and written
- Measurable progress and completion
- Achievable outcome
- Realistic in time and skill
- Time-based achievement

Goals Assessments

<u>Write down your goals for the different areas of life</u>

Goals Assessments (cont.)

<u>Where You Feel You're Currently At</u>

Our Stages Of Growth	Survival	Stability	Success	Significance
Personal				
Finance				
Business				
Spiritual				
Family				

Little Savings

Separating a little bit of saving each day can add up to quite a considerable amount in just a few years.
Below is an example of how little savings add up.

17 Cents per Day ($5 per month)	$60 saved in one year	$180 saved in three years	$600 saved in ten years
33 Cents per Day ($10 per month)	$120 saved in one year	$360 saved in three years	$1200 saved in ten years
83 Cents per Day ($25 per month)	$300 saved in one year	$900 saved in three years	$3000 saved in ten years
$1.66 Dollars per Day ($50 per month)	$600 saved in one year	$1800 saved in three years	$6000 saved in ten years

DREAM LINING EXAMPLE

FROM TIM FERRIS 4HOUR WORK WEEK

This tool puts everything you want and what it will take for you to get there in perspective. Fill out your own dream line and find out what it will take for you to live the way you want

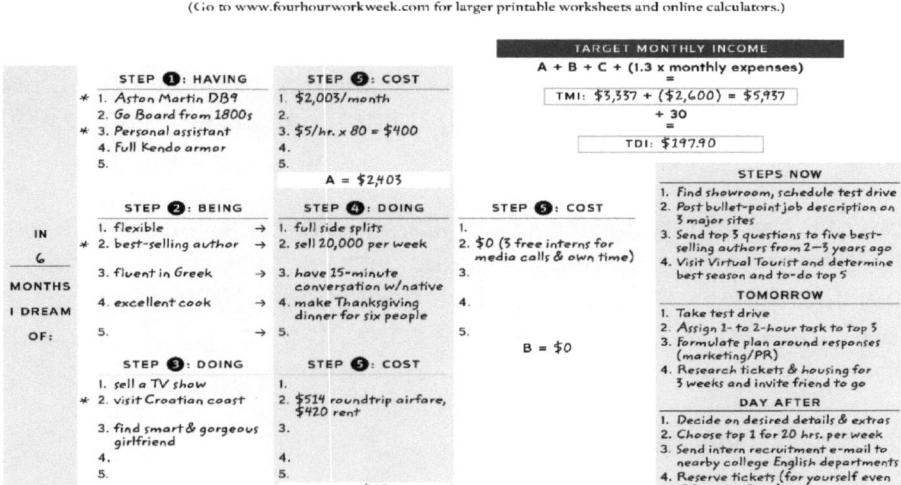

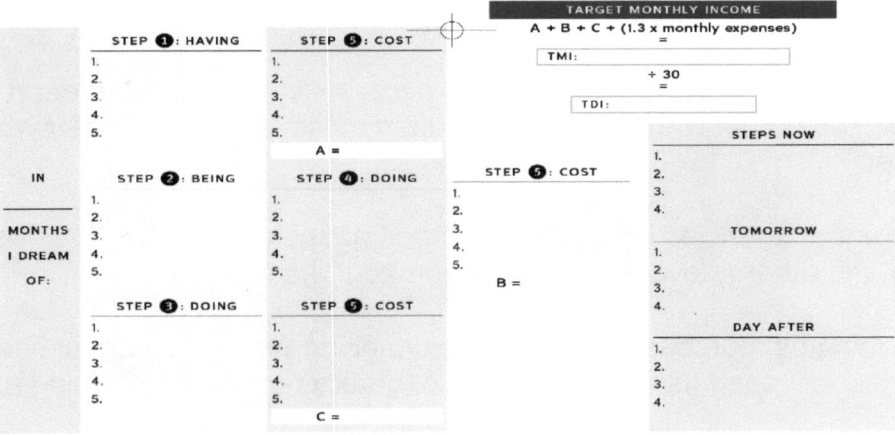

Important Income Considerations

- No need to have an LLC if you do not have at least $1 million worth of assets. (If you want an LLC or Corporation consult with a professional, some corporations have fees that need to be taken into consideration. In some cases, having a good insurance plan can provide great protection.)

- Maximize deductions: tools replacements, license fees, continuing education, supplies, smocks, gloves, car expenses, phone, home office, meals (who, when, where, why), mileage other than commuting to work, e.g. mileage travel to get supply.

- Home office = square footage of office/square footage of residence = x% Deduct x% from home expenses. Consult with your tax professional for additional information about home office deductions. 100% business use is RED FLAG for a home office because a percentage of your home is used for living.

- Deduct health insurance.

- Retirement: If you plan on using a retirement vehicle, make sure you accurately report your earnings, you do not want to raise a red flag by having more in savings vehicle than what you are reporting.

- If you plan on retiring, make sure to accurately and honestly report your income. You do not want to be caught up in messy paperwork later when you are older.

- Know that agencies like DMV and credit agencies report to IRS. Also, PayPal and other relevant services report your income too.

- For most big purchases that require financing through a conventional lender you will need to show 2-3 years of qualifying income. So plan ahead.

- Keeping your money under your mattress, in a safety deposit box, and bank accounts are common ways to secure your income.

- Know that some apartments will look at monthly bank statements or tax returns to qualify for housing. Each state is different but a lot have a mandate that with some apartment complexes. Certain number of units have to be allotted to those who qualify for low income, which could possibly be of great benefit when choosing a place to live.

- Know when trying to get a loan and you fail to qualify, you can look for possible hard money lenders (who lend money with less requirements at higher rates, and later you can refinance your loan with a conventional loan, if possible at lower rate.) Or find someone who will co-sign.

- Diversification research investments that interest you and have a portion going to one and a portion going to another

- Always have some money put aside to pay bills

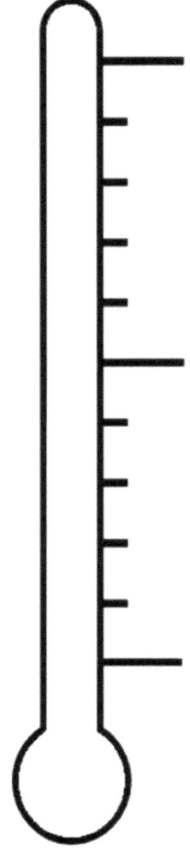

SAVINGS THERMOMETER

Investing

"Where do I invest my money?" I asked.
"The greatest investment you can make is the investment in yourself..." – Mr.W

There are a million ways to invest money and if you don't know what to do with it be sure there are people out there that are waiting to take it from you.

It all starts with you! You have to be first priority when it comes to your investment strategy. On one hand you got to invest wisely your time on those things that are most important to you like the preservation and care of your body. Before investing your money into things that you are not familiar with, invest in educating yourself on that topic(s). Once you invest the time learning about money, opportunities, and certain principles that apply to the preservation and multiplication of your money then you can confidently go into the direction that makes most since to you.

You will have to seek knowledge, and as you do you will find more and more info to help you. Listed in this chapter are some general definitions of investments that get tossed around a lot when money is concerned. An important thing to remember about any investment of time and capital, time being your biggest asset; what is the <u>return on your investment</u>. So if it is between investing in an IRA, buying a home or buying razors to sell, know your goals. Understand at different stages of your life both personal and business will require you to take action and make some type of investment to get what you want.

Know that there are reasons and benefits that most people don't see or take full advantage of in almost every type of investment. Get a knowledgeable CPA, and find out for yourself how to make the most out of your resources. Often times there are local meet-ups for all different types of investors so take advantage and go soak up as much information as possible.

Tip: *Invest in your passion. Don't let years go by watching other people get the success you dream about. It will be scary and your faith will be tested when you invest in you becoming the person you want to be; but, the reward of going for IT and achieving IT , makes IT all worth IT.*

STOCK, BONDS, TRUST AND MORE

BASIC INVESTING DEFINITIONS

ANNUITIES

Whether you're already retired or years away, you can feel more confident in your planning with guaranteed income from a fixed or variable annuity. An annuity can help provide a steady stream of income in retirement —which may help you maintain your standard of living and pursue the retirement lifestyle you want. Choose from fixed annuities with a stated payout rate, or variable annuities with a return based on market performance. Variable annuities offer tax-deferred growth potential, meaning investors pay no taxes on the earnings from the investments in the account until they receive payments or make withdrawals.

Benefits of Investing in Annuities

The only investment product that can provide guaranteed income for life, annuities are contracts between investors and insurance companies. Most annuities can grow tax-deferred and then provide regular payments for a set time period or for life. Some annuities make the same payment no matter what happens in the market. You can receive a steady stream of income, which can help you maintain your standard of living and enjoy the lifestyle you want.

Discover the Potential Advantages of Fixed-Income Investing

Fixed-income investments may be right for you if you want to experience these benefits as part of a diversified portfolio.

· **Preserve wealth** - While fixed-income prices may fluctuate, you can rely on receiving the full-face amount when your investment matures.

· **Diversify your portfolio** - Diversifying your investments across asset classes may result in less risk exposure for your overall portfolio

· **Generate income** - Fixed-income investments may provide a steady stream of monthly or quarterly income to help supplement your income or help fund your retirement

· **Manage interest rate risk** - By creating a ladder through staggered maturities, you can manage interest rate risk in both rising and falling environments and experience less exposure to interest rate volatility

Source -tdamirtrade.com

Bond

DEFINITION of 'Bond'

A bond is a debt investment in which an investor loans money to an entity (typically corporate or governmental) which borrows the funds for a defined period of time at a variable or fixed interest rate. Bonds are used by companies, municipalities, states and sovereign governments to raise money and finance a variety of projects and activities. Owners of bonds are debt holders, or creditors, of the issuer.

Source: Investopedia

Certificate Of Deposit - CD

DEFINITION of 'Certificate Of Deposit - CD'

A savings certificate entitling the bearer to receive interest. A CD bears a maturity date, a specified fixed interest rate and can be issued in any denomination. CD's are generally issued by commercial banks and are insured by the FDIC. The term of a CD generally ranges from one month to five years

Source: Investopedia

Dollar-Cost Averaging - DCA

DEFINITION of 'Dollar-Cost Averaging - DCA'

The technique of buying a fixed dollar amount of a particular investment on a regular schedule, regardless of the share price. More shares are purchased when prices are low, and fewer shares are bought when prices are high.

Also referred to as a "constant dollar plan."

Source: Investopedia

Irrevocable Trust

DEFINITION of 'Irrevocable Trust'

A trust that can't be modified or terminated without the permission of the beneficiary. The grantor, having transferred assets into the trust, effectively removes all of his or her rights of ownership to the assets and the trust

Land Trust

DEFINITION of 'Land Trust'

A legal agreement where a trustee is appointed to maintain ownership of a piece of real property for the benefit of another party: namely, the beneficiary of the trust. Land trusts are used by several different types of organizations for several reasons; nonprofit entities use them to hold conservation easements, and corporations and investment groups use them to accumulate large portions of land.

These agreements can also be known as Illinois-type land trusts.

Source: Investopedia

Lien Sale

DEFINITION of 'Lien Sale'

The sale of the claim or "hold" placed on an asset to satisfy an unpaid debt. Typically, lien sales are conducted as public auctions and the lien is on real estate, automobiles and other personal property. Depending on a particular state's laws, contractors, subcontractors and suppliers may put a lien on a piece of property they have worked on pending payment for services rendered.

Source: Investopedia

Mutual Fund

DEFINITION of 'Mutual Fund'

An investment vehicle that is made up of a pool of funds collected from many investors for the purpose of investing in securities such as stocks, bonds, money market instruments and similar assets. Mutual funds are operated by money managers, who invest the fund's capital and attempt to produce capital gains and income for the fund's investors. A mutual fund's portfolio is structured and maintained to match the investment objectives stated in its prospectus.

Source: Investopedia

Roth IRA

DEFINITION of 'Roth IRA'

An individual retirement plan that bears many similarities to the traditional IRA, but contributions are not tax deductible and qualified distributions are tax free. Similar to other retirement plan accounts, non-qualified distributions from a Roth IRA may be subject to a penalty upon withdrawal.

Source: Investopedia

Rule of 72

DEFINITION of 'Rule of 72'

A rule stating that in order to find the number of years required to double your money at a given interest rate, you divide the compound return into 72. The result is the approximate number of years that it will take for your investment to double.

BREAKING DOWN 'Rule of 72'

For example, if you want to know how long it will take to double your money at 12% interest, divide 12 into 72 and you get six years.

Source: Investopedia

Stock

DEFINITION of 'Stock'

A type of security that signifies ownership in a corporation and represents a claim on part of the corporation's assets and earnings.

There are two main types of stock: common and preferred. Common stock usually entitles the owner to vote at shareholders' meetings and to receive dividends. Preferred stock generally does not have voting rights, but has a higher claim on assets and earnings than the common shares. For example, owners of preferred stock receive dividends before common shareholders and have priority in the event that a company goes bankrupt and is liquidated.

Source: Investopedia

Simplified Employee Pension - SEP (Simplified Employee Pension IRA)

DEFINITION of 'Simplified Employee Pension - SEP (Simplified Employee Pension IRA)'

A retirement plan that an employer or self-employed individuals can establish. The employer is allowed a tax deduction for contributions made to the SEP plan and makes contributions to each eligible employee's SEP IRA on a discretionary basis.

Source: Investopedia

Tip: Research SEP IRA. Tools like SEP IRA gives you certain benefits when investing through your SEP IRA that you would not have investing personally, especially when purchasing investment property.

Trust

DEFINITION of 'Trust'

A fiduciary relationship in which one party, known as a trustor, gives another party, the trustee, the right to hold title to property or assets for the benefit of a third party, the beneficiary.

There are two types of trusts:
1. Living Trust (inter-vivos): A trust that is in effect during the trustor's lifetime.
2. Testamentary Trust: A trust that is created through the will of a deceased person.

Source: Investopedia

Core Lessons About Money:

- **Part of what you earn is yours to keep—Save 10%**
- **Control thy expenses**
- **Don't borrow unwisely or unnecessarily**
- **Make gold multiply—invest wisely and prudently**
- **Guard against loss—invest with a margin of safety**

- **Understand where you invest**

Source: The Richest Man In Babylon

Creating a New Product or Labeling an Existing Product

Having your own brand products is a great method of having your business known throughout the city and country. There is also a huge money-making potential behind selling your own brand products.

Creating a product is not some difficult or technical process. You can create even the most advanced and technical products with absolutely zero prior knowledge, and still be owner of a best-seller product. This is all done through outsourcing your work to capable individuals.

Have you ever noticed that even some of the most insignificant herbal clinics, massage spas, clothing stores etc. have their very own branded products? How? They can obviously never afford to create products by themselves, they have no industrial facility of their own.

The answer to that is that they are simply relabeling generic products to their brand name!

You too can create your very own brand product by having the generic products produced by relevant contractors and then label them to your brand name.
The three methods of creating your very own product are; **creating a product**, **licensing a product**, and **reselling a product**.

Creating a Product

Get in touch with skilled contractors and pitch them your idea, pay them to create your product. Then have it mass-produced according to your needs for selling to customers.

Licensing a Product

There are plenty of products who are already up for grabs from potential buyers. Simply purchase the license of these product and they are essentially yours. Outsource their production to reliable contractors and start selling.

Reselling a Product

You can also choose to simply purchase a generic product from contractors, label them as your own and start selling to your customers.

Difference between Broke and Poor

Being broke is a state of account. Being poor is a state of mind

Facts about the Rich

On average, they have:

- Been married for 28 years
- 3 children
- A net worth of 9.2 million
- A yearly income of $456,000
- A love for their work
- A strong spiritual faith
- Used their business to create wealth

Millionaires Top Ranking Success Factors

- Being well disciplined (habits)…57%
- Being honest with all people…57%
- Getting along with people…56%
- Having a supportive spouse…49%
- Working harder than most people…47%
- Loving their career/business…46%

- Having strong leadership qualities… 41%
- Having a very competitive spirit/personality…38%
- Being well organized…36%
- Having an ability to sell their ideas/products …35%
- Making wise investments…35%

Above all, they know how to live within their means.

The Sequence for Personal Financial Success

Follow these as guidelines for achieve great financial success in your personal life.

- Stability
- Success
- Significance

The Stability plan
- Have a working home budget
- Have a significantly sized life insurance policy
- Have a death will
- Have an automatic withdrawal into your savings accounts

The Success Plan
- Have financial and retirement plan
- Have living, revocable or irrevocable trust
- Have annual assessment of your net worth
- Have real estate and stock investments
- Have 3 to 6 month expenses in reserve

The Significance Plan

- Have passive investments that provide for your current lifestyle

- Have gifting strategies

The Sequence for Business Financial Success

Follow these as guidelines for achieve great financial success in your business life.

- Stability

- Success

- Significance

The Stability Plan
- Have a working business budget

- Have a fully funded retirement plan (SEP, IRA, RRSP)

- Have minimal three months' worth business expenses in reserve

The Success Plan
- Have a cash reserve to pay staff

- Have a tax strategy for deferment

- Make monthly Profit and Loss statements

The Significance Plan
- Have a plan in place for acquisition of your business

- Have a profit sharing plan

- Make cuts at home first

- Invest in your business

- Invest in yourself

- Know the real score

- Get check ahead

- Pay yourself a salary

Financial Assessment Guide

You can also assess your financial worth through following instructions below:

- List out all bank accounts numbers with their balance
- List out all debt (other than real estate) with balances, interest rates and payments
- Are you covered? Assemble all insurance policies
- List out beneficiary amounts and premium payments
- List total amount of any cash balances/ surrender value

Retirement Analysis

- List total value of 401k, RRSP or SEP accounts
- List total value of any other retirement vehicles
- Analyze 12-month history of retirement investment ROR
- List out all your real estate holdings, including

    a. Monthly payments and interest rates

    b. Loan balances

    c. Approximate current values

    d. Equity on each property

Now you have a complete overview of your personal and business financing. Persistency and care, connecting, and service recording will give you accurate details of your barbering business.

HEALTH

Staying Healthy

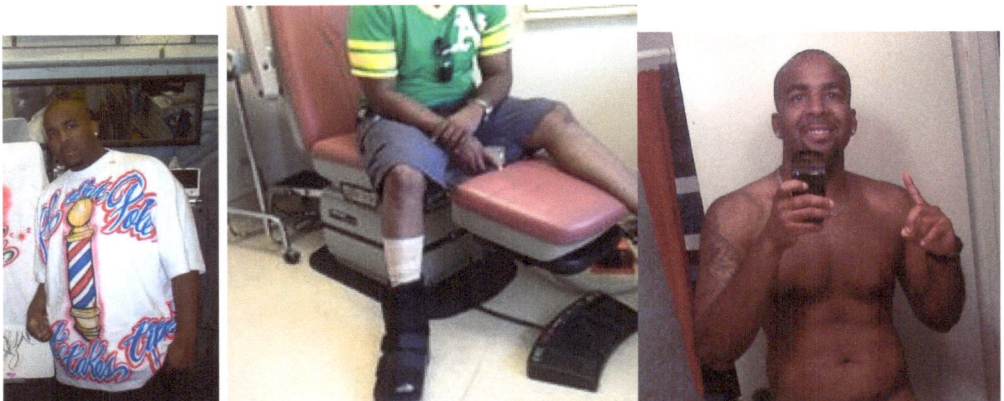

Years of overweight me @275lbs-Injured Foot Fractured-Me at 175lbs

I cannot stress to you enough that you have to take care of your body. You love cutting hair and want to cut, and possibly retire healthy and on your own terms not because health issues held you back. I am talking about taking care of yourself mentally and physically.

Mentally

Listening and talking to so many people about life issues can be very draining overtime. You are like a psychologist and sometimes people throw their emotional weight on you, your sympathy or people going through different trials can affect your energy.

It effects how you interact with the next client, the people you work with, and your family and spouse. You must not let every story you hear effect you internally or your mind will overload and you will not be able to give the proper care and attention to others.

It is very important that you take mental breaks TOO! Try to make sure that whatever you choose is a healthy choice. I used to smoke cigars on breaks which was a terrible choice because it is not healthy and you smell like smoke the rest of the day. Now I just take a short walk or find a quiet place to rest and gather my thoughts and keep my focus.

Find an activity that relieves stress and is fun for you. Exercise is also great but sometimes you need something more enjoyable like playing a game, reading a book, or visiting a beautiful place.

Physically

Understand that you put your body through a lot, I have experienced pain in my hands and wrist from holding clippers and cutting all day long. Shoulder pain and lower back pain from standing all day with bad support. Bad posture, a weak core, and putting myself in awkward cutting positions. I also had my right foot fractured in three places and degenerative bone loss in my left foot from extended periods of standing on my feet, being overweight, having bad foot support, then ignoring the problem by just icing my feet and taking a pain reliever. See the list of exercises below.

Diet

You got to eat to keep going and a lot of barbers do not plan their meals and they suffer for it. They make bad decision on what they put into their body. You got to meal plan!

Pack a lunch; vegetables, beans/legumes, and protein. Then have healthy snacks like Fruit or Nuts. Also drink plenty of water. You are no good when you are hungry so make sure you prepare well.

Weight and fitness in the past was always a big challenge for me. I lost over 95lbs eating right and doing light exercises. You can too! Incorporate healthy habits into your diet and you will add years of longevity to your career, while also avoiding painful injuries. I also found that a good massage also helps a lot with reliving stress and tension.

Weight Loss

If you are someone like me weight loss can be very challenging. You look around everywhere for help and advice. You ask people what they eat how they work out and spend money trying new diets or supplements that are supposed to help you either slim down or put on muscle. I commend your efforts, but if you're like me none of that worked.

To start, you find some diet and in your mind you're reading this menu of foods and portion sizes and you are already unhappy. Someone either gives you a workout plan or you find a gym partner and after a few workouts your sore, starving, and confidence is lowered because you haven't lost an inch. You spend your days craving every food that's featured on all the televisions commercials you watch in the shop. Images of juicy hamburgers falling in slow motion makes your mouth water. You start thinking about the alternative that you brought from home and your spinach and beans salad just doesn't match up to what you are really craving.

Soon you abandon the diet, stop going to the gym and back into your bad habits.
I lived this cycle for years! Sure there were times I went hard in the gym to get ready for summer or to get in shape by my birthday, but I usually would end up injuring myself or just be discourage because I could not reach my goals in the set time and I would give up.

Other things in life caused problems to when it came to weight loss, after my grandmother died of cancer, I was very depressed and I ate a lot of high fat, high carb, high sodium foods. If it was meaty and cheesy I was eating it.
Dating was another thing that caused a lot of weight to be gained. Going out to eat, then to get some drinks night after night did a lot of damage. There was something irresistible about steak fries at two thirty in the morning that would cause me pick up some before heading home.

This is what I found…

While diets and exercise plans are great if you can stop your bad habits and go comfortably into a healthy regiment. I couldn't do it overnight, it took time and I had to wean myself away from the bad habits and develop new habits gradually.

This is what you do:

Take a current inventory of your favorite bad foods or snacks
How many times a week are you eating them?
How often do you get some physical activity per week?
How often do you call yourself fat or talk negatively about yourself?

The key here is that you are going to be making changes for life so you can grow into good habits.

Set goals for small improvements each week. Example: instead of eating fast food seven times a week I will this week only eat fast food six times and in two weeks I will drop down to five times and so on and so on. Instead of not working out at all. In the morning I will walk around my block one time before heading to work. In two week's time I will walk around the block twice and so on and so on keep getting better.

What you tell yourself about you affects how you think about you and the results you'll see.

I one hundred pounds and still thought I was fat at times. I had spent so many years being big, being fat became part of my identity and perception of myself. Year after year people take this to the extreme and do all type of damaging things to their body. Avoid the pitfalls of a negative mentality by being encouraging to yourself. **"Every day in every way I am getting better and better"** should be on repeat in your head.

Mentally it takes being on your team. You have to be your biggest encourager, your loudest fan, you have to reward yourself and celebrate your victories. Will it be challenging? Yes, it will. Will it be worth it? Hell yes.

Rather it's losing weight starting a business, perfecting a skill or any other type of change you will have to be completely sold out on you and have faith that the actions you take every day will bring you closer to your goals.

As you journey down the path to your dreams there will be examples and resources of what has worked for other people. Find or create a model that will get you the result you want and then once you reached that goal look for a better model to get you to that next level.

One of the hardest thing to do at the shop for a barber is to eat right. A busy schedule of clients will cause most barbers not to eat or to make poor food choices. To have a healthy diet and insure that you have good healthy food on hand you have to meal prep.
TIP: *Some meats like chicken after being cook have a limited amount of days that it will be good and safe to consume so as a rule of thumb try to prepare your meats for 3 days of consumption.*

What you need:
6 plastic containers w/lids -Try to find microwavable safe
2 packs of boneless skinless chicken breast - Total of 12 pieces
1 bag of baby spinach
1 can of black beans
1 can of pinto beans
1 bag of carrots
Seasoning - natural seasoning herbs are great to use like thyme and rosemary

Meal Prep

Steps:
Season chicken
Put in oven 350 degrees for about 30mins
Divide spinach, chicken and beans into your plastic container
TIP: Get a meat thermometer to make sure all your meat is fully cooked

List of Low Glycemic Foods

This is important to pay attention too, because even though some foods are healthy, how quickly they enter the blood stream and raise your glucose levels, then the body can either use for energy or store for fat can affect your weight loss goals. So knowing what to eat to best fuel you through a day of cutting hair is important.

On this list the low glycemic carbs that are carb dense and would therefore have a high glycemic load have an asterisk *after them. Don't eat more than 1 serving per meal and for most people no more than 2 servings a day.
FRUIT:
Apple
Kiwi
Applesauce
Lemon
Blueberries

Lime
Blackberries
Mandarin Oranges
Boysenberries
Nectarine
Raspberries
Orange
Gooseberries
Peach
Strawberries
Pear
Casaba melon
Persimmon
Honeydew melon
Plum
Cherries
Pomegranate
Figs
Tangerine
Grapes
Tangelo

*Mangos and papayas could be low glycemic if they are not over ripe. These fruits canned in water with no sugar added are low glycemic. No more than 1/2 cup unsweetened 100% pure fruit juice mixed with water (pulp lowers glycemic response.)

VEGETABLES:
Artichoke
Leeks
Arugula
Lettuce
Asparagus
Mushrooms
Avocado
Okra
Garbanzo Beans
Onions
Beans, lime
Olives
Bean sprouts
Peas, dried, green or split
Black eyed peas
Pickles
Broccoli
Radishes
Brussels sprouts

Sauerkraut
Cabbage
Scallions
Cauliflower
Snow peas
Celery
Spinach
Collard greens
Squash, summer yellow
Eggplant
Sweet potatoes, yams
Endive
Tomatoes
Escarole
Turnip greens
Bell peppers, red, yellow, green
Water chestnuts
Kale
Watercress
Kohlrabi
Zucchini

*Beets, carrots and winter squash are nutrient dense and are not starchy vegetables. Beets have a moderate index. All other vegetables are low glycemic and should be consumed as juice.

Half your plate should be vegetables and fruits each meal.
100% whole grain breads
The more whole grains and seeds in the bread the lower the index.

Sprouted grain breads (some brands are Ezekiel, Alvarado St. Bakery, Food for Life - available in natural food stores or on the internet.) *

Sprouted grain tortillas (same)*
100% whole wheat tortillas*
100% whole grain cereals* hot and cold (no sugar or additives added, made out of the whole grain like bran, muesli, buckwheat.) *
Oatmeal*
Pastas*
Quinoa pasta (high protein) *
Barilla pasta (yellow box is high protein) *
All dry pasta is low glycemic but the high protein and whole grain pastas have an even lower glycemic index. Do not overcook.
Whole Grains*
Barley*
Quinoa*
Bulgur*

Buckwheat kasha*
Rye*
100% whole wheat flour made with unrefined, unprocessed whole wheat flour. *
100% whole grain pancake mixes* may be low glycemic

Rice is generally high glycemic but if you can find parboiled, high amylose rice this one has the lowest index. Amylose is the type of starch in the rice and it is soluble. You don't want sticky rice. Using a rice cooker helps. Also chilled rice as in rice rolls makes it resistant starch and a lower glycemic index. *
Eggs from free range chickens are best.
Fish
Chicken
Turkey
Wild game
Beef free range, grass fed is best.
Lamb
Pork
Dairy products (with no added sugar or high glycemic additives) yogurt, kefir, sour cream, cream cheese, crème fraiche, cheeses, milk, cream, buttermilk.
Beans (except for fava and broad beans) *
Nuts (unsalted is best for weight management and to avoid excess sodium,) 7 nuts is a serving and for weight management no more than 2 servings a day at different meals is best.
Nut and seed milks that are unsweetened like almond milk, coconut milk, hazelnut milk, hemp seed milk. Soy milk is high glycemic unless you buy unsweetened.
Seeds (a few salted ok in a salad but best unsalted for snacking,) pumpkin, sesame, sunflower, chia, hemp.
Nut and Seed Butters
Peanut butter
Almond butter
Cashew butter
Tahini (sesame seed butter)
All nut butters are low glycemic but only if they are 100% nuts or seeds with no added sugar or high glycemic additives.
Oils
Cold pressed **olive oil**
Expeller pressed **coconut oil**
Unrefined, cold pressed **seed and nut oils**
Butter
Sweeteners
Coconut palm sugar
Truvia
Stevia
Agave syrup
Erythritol
Xylitol.

Spices and seasonings with no sugar or high glycemic additives.
Salsa, taco and picante sauce are low glycemic unless they contain high glycemic additives.
Salad dressings when made without sugar or high glycemic additives.

Make your own or order just vinegar and oil in a restaurant. Restaurants always use dressings with high glycemic preservatives because they need the shelf life.

Coffee and tea can be high glycemic because caffeine increases insulin secretion. If they have high antioxidant content they could be low glycemic. Look for specifically formulated coffees and drink green tea made from tea leaves.

Jams and jellies are low glycemic if they are made from low glycemic fruits and have no added sugar or high glycemic additives.

Proteins and fats are low glycemic. However, eating too much animal protein at a meal can raise blood sugar. One serving of protein is enough for one meal. The healthiest proteins for people are plant proteins, like nuts, seeds, nut butters, seed butters, legumes, whole grains and soy beans.

The healthiest animal proteins are eggs, dairy products (unsweetened, low fat) fish, poultry and wild game.

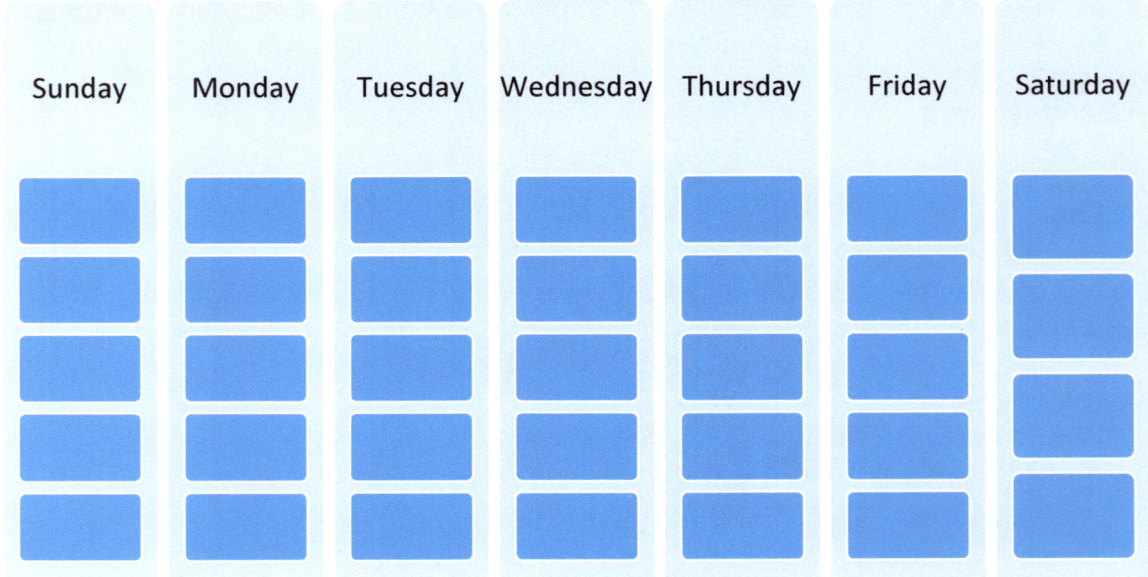

Managing Fatigue and Aches

You are only as old as you feel, the saying goes. But what if you feel old, tired, and rundown? Fatigue is a common complaint, especially after people hit middle age. Fortunately, there are plenty of simple ways to boost energy. Some even slow the aging process for barbers.
Here's how to refill your tank when your energy levels sputter.

Rule out Health Problems

Fatigue is a common symptom of many illnesses, including diabetes, heart disease and many more. Many medications can contribute to fatigue. These include some blood pressure medicines, antihistamines, diuretics, and other drugs. If you begin to experience fatigue after starting a new medication, tell your doctor.

Get Moving

The last thing you may feel like doing when you are tired is exercising. But many studies show that physical activity boosts energy levels.
"Exercise has consistently been linked to improved vigor and overall quality of life," says Kerry J. Stewart, professor of medicine and director of clinical and research exercise physiology at Johns Hopkins University School of Medicine. "People who become active have a greater sense of self-confidence. But exercise also improves the working efficiency of your heart, lungs, and muscles," Stewart says. "That's the equivalent of improving the fuel efficiency of a car. It gives you more energy for any kind of activity."

Strike a Pose

Although almost any exercise is good, yoga may be especially effective for boosting energy. After six weeks of once-a-week yoga classes, volunteers in a British study reported improvements in clear-mindedness, energy, and confidence.

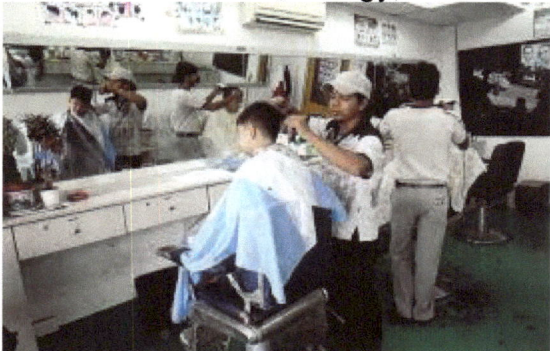

Best Lighting

Fluorescent lights dissipated the light better than other lighting would. Of course recessed lights would be recommended if they are possible. There are surface mount

Fluorescent lights available with a very low profile. Installing the lights on the top of the wall all around the room could be another possibility. Perhaps strips of fluorescent lights between mirror panels.

What Products Help

As you get older, health advice like "Drink your milk to grow big and strong" gives way to "Take your calcium pills to avoid osteoporosis." Taking your vitamins is especially important post 50, "as the absorption of nutrients and minerals and vitamins can decline," explained Dr. Mickey Barber, president of Cenegenics Carolinas. "We don't absorb as efficiently as we once did."
While eating can be a great way to get the vitamins and minerals our bodies need for optimum cell function, it's impossible to get all of them from every meal. "Unless you're growing your own food and it's all organic, pesticide and hormone free, you cook all your own meals [and] you never eat out," Barber said, "you're going to need at least a multivitamin."

Supplements

Supplements are great addition to your diet. Using supplements will help ensure that any shortcomings in your food are fulfilled effectively. They can be in form of pills or drinks; use whatever type of supplement you think is best for you.

- Herbal Supplements
- Protein Supplements
- Homeopathic Supplements
- Multivitamin Pills
- Fruit Drinks

Neck Stiffness

Barbers get much more neck and shoulder pain and problems in their forearms and wrists than average. Standing up for long periods, holding your arms up in the air while doing intricate repetitive movements can cause aches and pains. In fact, over half of Barbers get neck and shoulder pain and nearly 2/3 get back pain. If you are a Barber what can you do about it?

Typically, neck and shoulder pain in Barbers is caused by muscle tension and locking of the joints of the spine. This may lead to Cervical Facet Joint Syndrome. Here the joints of the neck become stiff and inflamed and can lead to nerve irritation. Some nerves coming out of the neck go down the arms to control the muscles in the wrist and hand. Problems in the neck can cause muscle weakness, pins and needles and pain.

The muscles of the shoulders and arms are not designed to contract for long periods. Instead, they are much better at short periods of intense activity followed by a break. Holding your arms up with the muscles tensed, decreases the blood flow and may lead to tissue damage. It is thought that this is one potential mechanism for repetitive strain injury.

Movements to be avoided

Proper neck posture, a simple matter of good body mechanics, can offer you protection from neck pain. Here are suggestions from the American Academy of Physical Medicine and Rehabilitation and other experts that can help prevent the misuse or overuse of your neck:

1. Do not sit or stand at your workstation. If you are stuck at your station, place items around your office so that you are forced to get up or stretch to get them.

2. Maintain good posture for your neck. Adjust your cutting chair so your hips are slightly higher than your knees. Your head and neck will then naturally assume the correct position. Also adjust your seat with each client so the height is optimal for you.

3. Do not sleep with too many pillows or with a pillow that's too thick. It may cause further stiffness or pain.

4. When talking on the phone, do not cradle the phone between head and shoulder. If you're on the phone often, switch to a headset or speakerphone.

5. If you have corrected vision, keep your prescription current so you don't have to crane your neck forward to see clearly.

Stretches or Exercise

Top tips for preventing neck, shoulder and arm pain

1. Get to work early. If you arrive in a rush, puffed out from running up the street, your muscles will be tense before you even start work. If you are calm and relaxed, your muscles will be too. Also, you will have time to do Tip 2.

2. Do a few simple stretches before you start working.

3. Take a mini break every few minutes. Every few minutes. Let your hands drop

your sides and shake loose to relax the muscles.

4. In between clients do a couple of the stretching exercises again and massage your neck, shoulder and forearm muscles.

5. Perch on a high stool when you can. This eases the pressure on your lower back and feet.

6. Avoid raising your arms up so high by lowering the clients chair or standing on a platform.

7. Keep your wrists straight. If your wrists are held at odd angles you are straining your forearm muscles.

8. Breathe deeply. This improves the oxygen supply to your muscles and helps keep them relaxed. If you're tense and breathing shallowly your muscles are more likely to go into spasm.

9. Do not smoke. People who smoke get more aches and pains in their muscles and joints. If you drink, take it easy. Some of the chemicals in alcoholic drinks increase inflammation.

10. At the end of the work day do the simple stretches again.

If you are still getting aches and pains, go and see a chiropractors and massage therapists who can help you.

Best Posture

The muscles in your neck can be exercised and strengthened just like other muscles in your body. Plus, exercise will improve your neck's range of motion. Make sure you check with your health care provider before doing neck exercises. Stop at once if any movement causes you pain.

Before you begin a neck exercise, it is important to find the proper starting position for your head. This helps prevent exercise-related injuries. Do this by putting your head squarely over your shoulders, then move it straight forward and then back. This back or base position is your starting point. For each of the following exercises, begin with 5 repetitions and build up to 10.

Exercise

Rotations. Head Up > Down, Side > Side, looking to your right, place right hand on forehead and stretch lightly. Hold for 10 to 15 seconds.
Looking down to the left, use right hand to cradle head under the occipital bone, raise back of the head up stretching neck as you continue to look down.

Back Pain

A back muscle strain or ligament strain is one of the most common causes of acute lower back pain. Lifting a heavy object, twisting, or a sudden movement can cause muscles or ligaments stretch or develop microscopic tears. With a lower back strain, the severity of the pain ranges from mild discomfort to severe, disabling pain, depending on the extent of strain and the lower back muscle spasms that result from the injury.

Chronic lower back pain worsened by certain positions and movements.
Symptoms may include any combination of the following:
1. Low-level of constant lower back pain punctuated by episodes of severe pain/muscle spasms lasting a few days to a few months

2. Chronic pain that can range from nagging to severe

3. Back pain worsened by sitting

4. Walking, even running, may feel better than sitting/standing. This is especially recommended for days you receive high volume of clients.

5. Changing positions frequently relieves pain

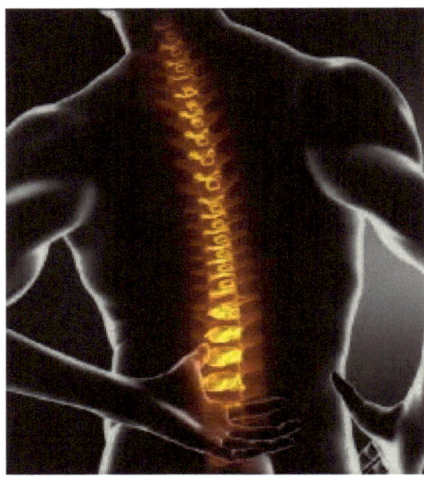

How to prevent or lessen strain?
Most cases of low back pain do not require urgent care, but anyone should see a doctor immediately if low back pain is a result of trauma, or if pain is accompanied by any of the following symptoms:

1. Fever and chills

2. Unexplained recent weight loss

3. Significant leg weakness

4. Sudden bowel and/or bladder incontinence—either difficulty passing urine or having a bowel movement, or loss of control of urination or bowel movement

5. Severe, continuous abdominal pain

STRECHES AND EXERCISE

Supine Hamstring Stretch

Lying on your back, bend your right knee into your chest and place a strap or rolled-up towel around the ball of your foot. Straighten your leg toward the ceiling. Press out through both heels. If the lower back feels strained, bend the left knee and place the foot on the ground Hold for 3-5 minutes and then switch to the left let for 3-5 minutes.

Two-Knee Twist

Lying on your back, bend your knees into your chest and bring your arms out at a T. As you exhale lower your knees to ground on the right. Keep both shoulders pressing down firmly. If the left shoulder lifts, lower your knees further away from the right arm. Hold for 1-2 minutes each side.

Products to use

Low back strain can be a painful and depressing injury. But the good news is that most cases heal on their own, given time. To speed the healing, you should:

1. **Ice your back** to reduce pain and swelling as soon as you injure yourself. Do it for 20-30 minutes every 3-4 hours for 2-3 days. You can also ice your back after physical activity.

2. **Apply heat to your back but only after 2-3 days of icing it first.** Use heat on your back only after the initial swelling has gone down. You could use an electric heating pad or a hot water bottle. Or you could just soak in a hot bath.

3. **Take painkillers or other drugs,** if recommended by your doctor. Non-steroidal anti-inflammatory drugs will help with lower back pain and swelling. However, these drugs may have side effects. They should be used only occasionally, unless your doctor specifically says otherwise. Prescription painkillers and muscle relaxants are sometimes necessary.

4. **Use support.** Ask your doctor or therapist first, but consider getting a belt or girdle to add support to your back. Use it only short-term or for support with heavy or repetitive lifting.

5. **Get physical therapy** to build up strength, if your doctor recommends it. Do not stay in bed or on the couch all day. That will make it worse.

6. **Maintain good muscle tone** in your abdominal and lower back muscles. No matter what people tell you, bed rest does not work. People used to think that the best treatment for low back strain was to lie on your back until you felt better. But studies show it does not help. In fact, after taking it easy for a day or two, you should usually start light physical activity.

Feet Strain

Exercises Stretch and Strengthen.

1. With the feet flat on the floor, press the toes downwards into the floor.
2. Do not allow them to curl, or the ankle to move whilst performing the exercise.
3. Hold for the count of 3, repeat 10 times.
4. Perform this exercise 3 times a day if possible.
5. Progress the exercise by holding the contraction for longer.

Spreading the toes

1. Place feet flat on the floor.
2. Spread the toes as far as they will go and then return them together.
3. Repeat this 10 times, rest and perform a further 2 sets of 10 repetitions.
4. Aim to repeat this exercise 3 times a day, as above.

Forefoot press

1. Place the back half of a foot on a suitable book, and the forefoot on a set of weighing scales, ensuring the foot is horizontal as far as possible.
2. Press down with the forefoot onto the scales to see who much force you generate.
3. Repeat 10 times for each foot.
4. Perform these exercises daily. It is an excellent way of seeing exactly how the strength of the foot is improving.

Toe lifting

1. Place feet flat on the floor and try to lift each toe up in turn.
2. Aim to keep the others flat on the floor - not easy, is it?
3. Perform three sets of each toe.
4. Try to perform this exercise twice a day - at least once.

Pencil lifting

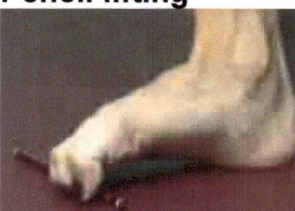

1. Pick up a pencil in the toes.
2. Hold for count of 6, repeat 10 times.
3. Aim to perform this exercise 3 times a day.
4. An alternative version of this is to repeatedly scrunch up a towel in the toes.

Walking on the toes

1. Simply walk about on tip toe.
2. Do not wear shoes but perform the exercise barefoot.
3. Aim for 8 sets of 15 to 20 seconds with 20 seconds rest between.
4. Complete the exercise 2 times a day. Progress by increasing the duration of the walks.

Walking on the heels

1. As above but walk on the heels.
2. Aim for 8 sets of 15 to 20 seconds with 20 seconds rest between.
3. Complete the exercise 2 times a day. Progress by increasing the duration of the walks.

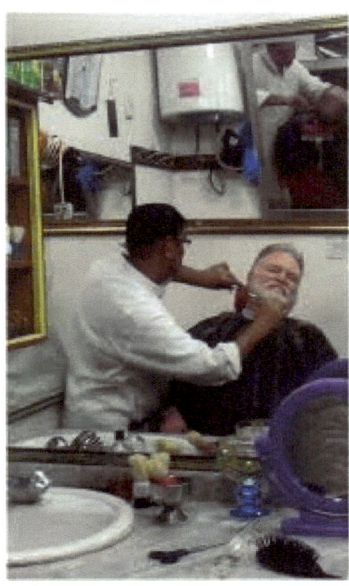

How often should they be rested throughout the day?

Standing for more than 2 hours at a time is now mildly uncomfortable. You should take a rest at less every one hour thirty minute.

Foot Wear is the best

Consider purchasing thick insole shoes that provide good ankle support. Remember to replace your shoes every three to six months.

What shoes should be Avoided?

1. Thin Sole Shoes

2. Dress shoes with no support.

3. Low support, low profile casual shoes

Hand Stiffness

Cause of stiffness in fingers and wrist

1. Is caused by pressure on a nerve (median nerve) in the wrist. The symptoms include tingling, numbness, weakness, or pain of the fingers and hand.

2. Tendon pain is actually a symptom of tendinitis, a series of very small tears (micro tears) in the tissue in or around the tendon. In addition to pain and tenderness, common symptoms of tendon injury include decreased strength and

movement in the affected area.

3. De quatrain's disease can occur in the hand and wrist when tendons and the tendon covering (sheath) on the thumb side of the wrist swell and become inflamed. See a picture of De quatrain's disease.

4. Repetitive motion syndrome is a term used to describe symptoms such as pain, swelling, or tenderness that occur from repeating the same motion over and over.

5. Writer's cramps develop with repeated hand or finger motion, such as writing or typing.

6. Trigger finger or trigger thumb occurs when the flexor tendon and its sheath in a finger or thumb thicken or swell.

7. Dupuytren's disease is an abnormal thickening of tissue beneath the skin in the palm of the hand or hands and occasionally the soles of the feet. The thickened skin and tendons (palmar fascia) may eventually limit movement or cause the fingers to bend so that they can't be straightened. See a picture of Dupuytren's contractor.

8. Ganglion cysts are small sacs (cysts) filled with clear, jellylike fluid that often appear as bumps on the hands and wrists but can also develop on feet, ankles, knees, or shoulders. See a picture of a Ganglion.

Cause of hands vibrating sensation after cutting has stopped

You are cutting your client's hair, trying to ignore the tingling or numbness you have had for months in your hand and wrist. Suddenly, a sharp, piercing pain shoots through the wrist and up your arm. Just a passing cramp? More likely you have carpal tunnel syndrome, a painful progressive condition caused by compression of a key nerve in the wrist.

What are the symptoms of carpal tunnel syndrome? Symptoms usually start gradually, with frequent burning, tingling, or itching numbness in the palm of the hand and the fingers, especially the thumb and the index and middle fingers. Decreased grip strength may make it difficult to form a fist, grasp small objects, or perform other manual tasks. In chronic and/or untreated cases, the muscles at the base of the thumb may waste away. Some people are unable to tell between hot and cold by touch.

What are the causes of carpal tunnel syndrome? Carpal tunnel syndrome is often the result of a combination of factors that increase pressure on the median nerve and tendons in the carpal tunnel, rather than a problem with the nerve itself. Most likely the disorder is due to a congenital predisposition – the carpal tunnel is simply smaller in some people than in others. Other contributing factors include trauma or injury to the wrist that cause swelling, such as sprain or fracture; over activity of the pituitary gland;

hypothyroidism; rheumatoid arthritis; mechanical problems in the wrist joint; work stress; repeated use of vibrating hand tools; fluid retention during pregnancy or menopause; or the development of a cyst or tumor in the canal.

Writer's cramp – a condition in which a lack of fine motor skill coordination and ache and pressure in the fingers, wrist, or forearm is brought on by repetitive activity.

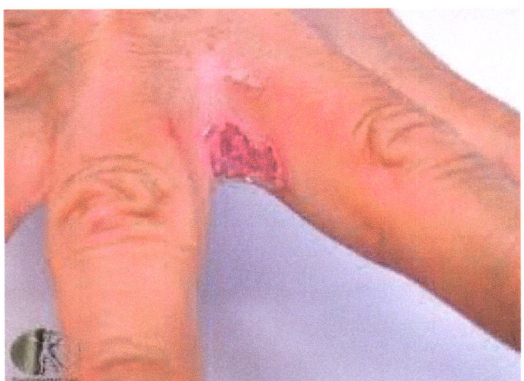

Stretches and Exercises

Stretching and strengthening exercises can be helpful in people whose symptoms have abated. These exercises may be supervised by a physical therapist, who is trained to use exercises to treat physical impairments, or an occupational therapist, who is trained in evaluating people with physical impairments and helping them build skills to improve their health and well-being.

At the barbershop, workers can do on-the-job conditioning, perform stretching exercises, take frequent rest breaks, wear splints to keep wrists straight, and use correct posture and wrist position. Wearing fingerless gloves can help keep hands warm and flexible. Workstations, tools and tool handles, and tasks can be redesigned to enable the worker's wrist to maintain a natural position during work. Jobs can be rotated among workers. Employers can develop programs in ergonomics, the process of adapting workplace conditions and job demands to the capabilities of workers. However, research has not conclusively shown that these workplace changes prevent the occurrence of carpal tunnel syndrome.

Products to Help

Drugs – Consult with your doctor first. In special circumstances, various drugs can ease the pain and swelling associated with carpal tunnel syndrome. Non-steroidal anti-inflammatory drugs, such as aspirin, ibuprofen, and other non-prescription pain relievers, may ease symptoms that have been present for a short time or have been caused by strenuous activity. Orally administered diuretics ("water pills") can decrease swelling. Corticosteroids (such as prednisone) or the drug lidocaine can be injected directly into the wrist or taken by mouth (in the case of prednisone) to relieve pressure on the median nerve and provide immediate, temporary relief to persons with mild or intermittent symptoms. (Caution: persons with diabetes and those who may be predisposed to diabetes should note that prolonged use of corticosteroids can make it difficult to regulate insulin levels. Corticosteroids should not be taken without a doctor's prescription.) Additionally, some studies show that vitamin B6 (pyridoxine) supplements may ease the symptoms of carpal tunnel syndrome.

Stretches

Follow these stretch pattern to shake off the stress and give your body the health boost it needs. Full description of stretches and exercises visit www.betheworldsgreatestbarber.com

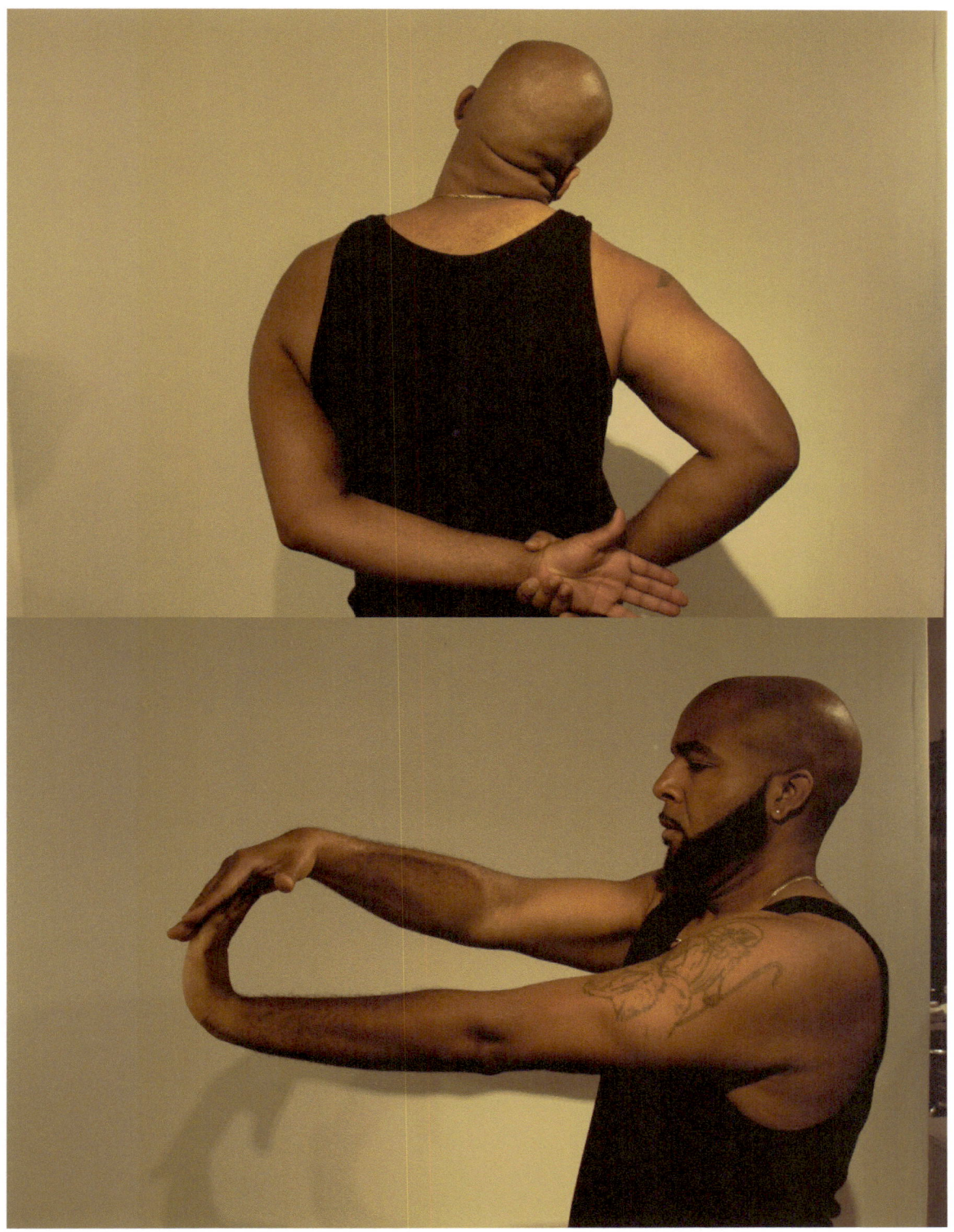

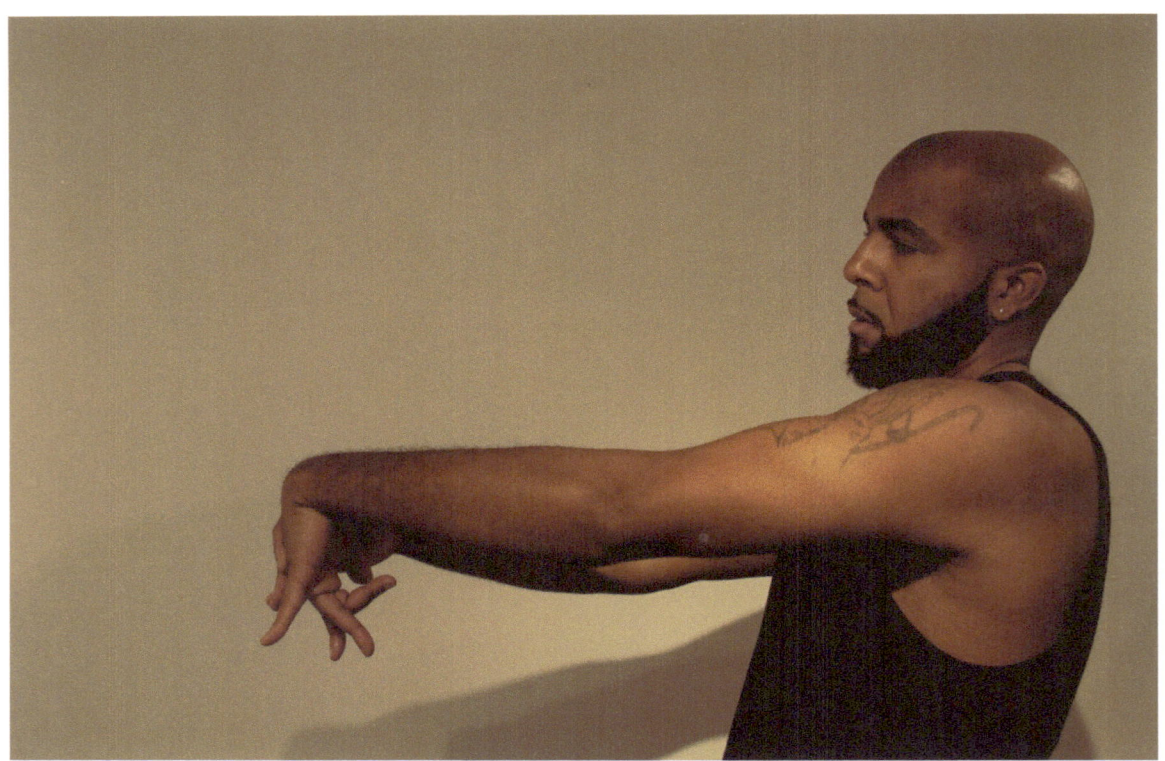

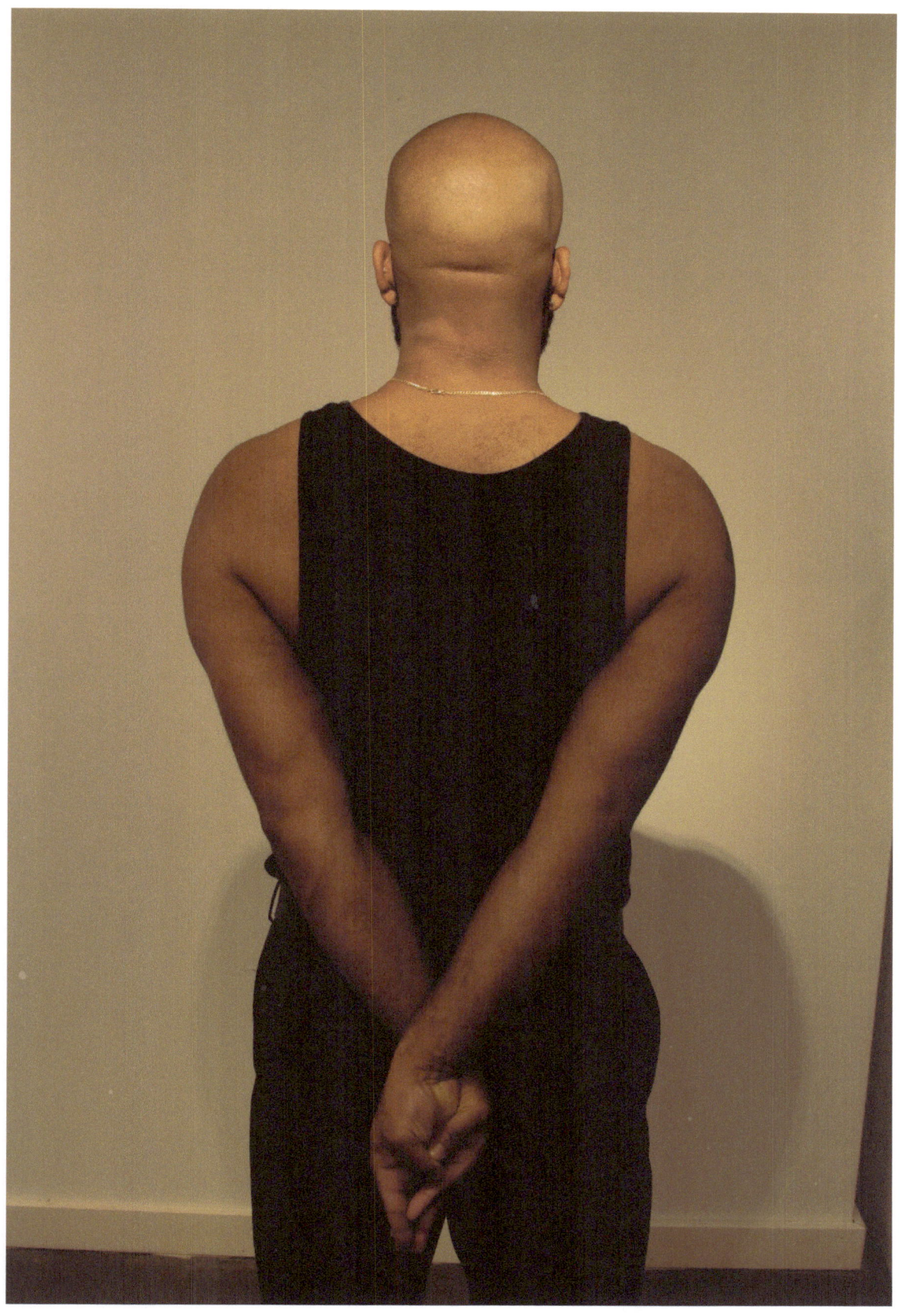

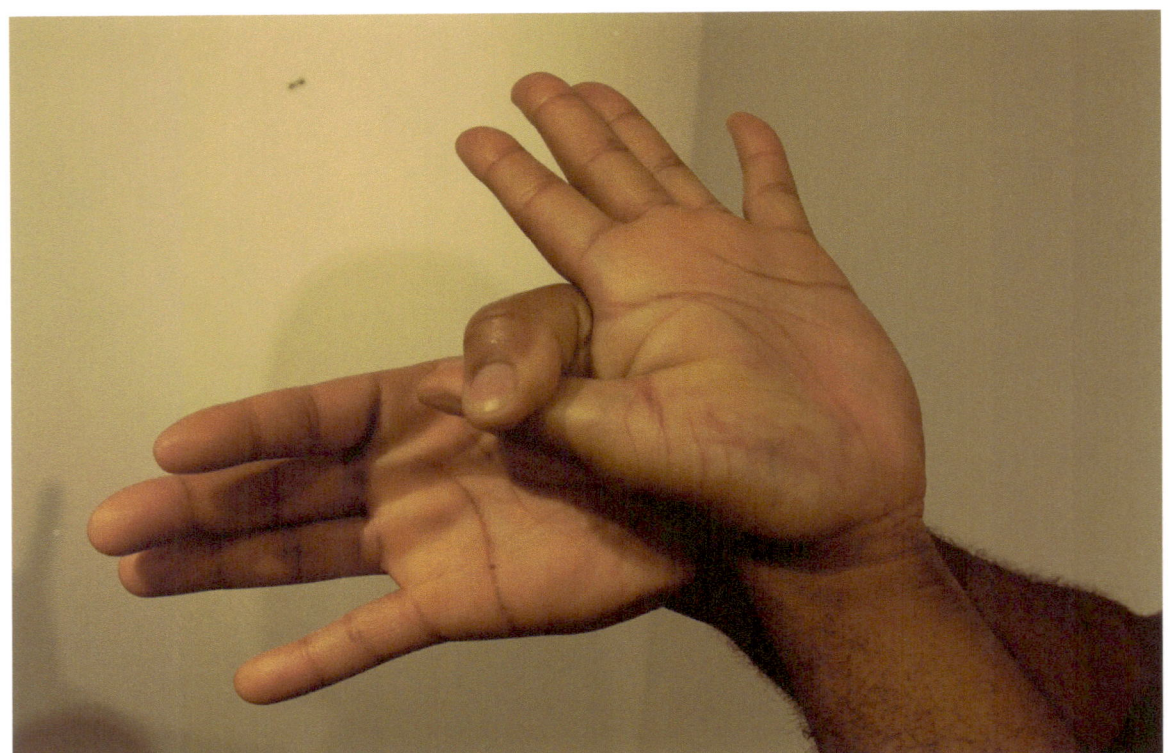

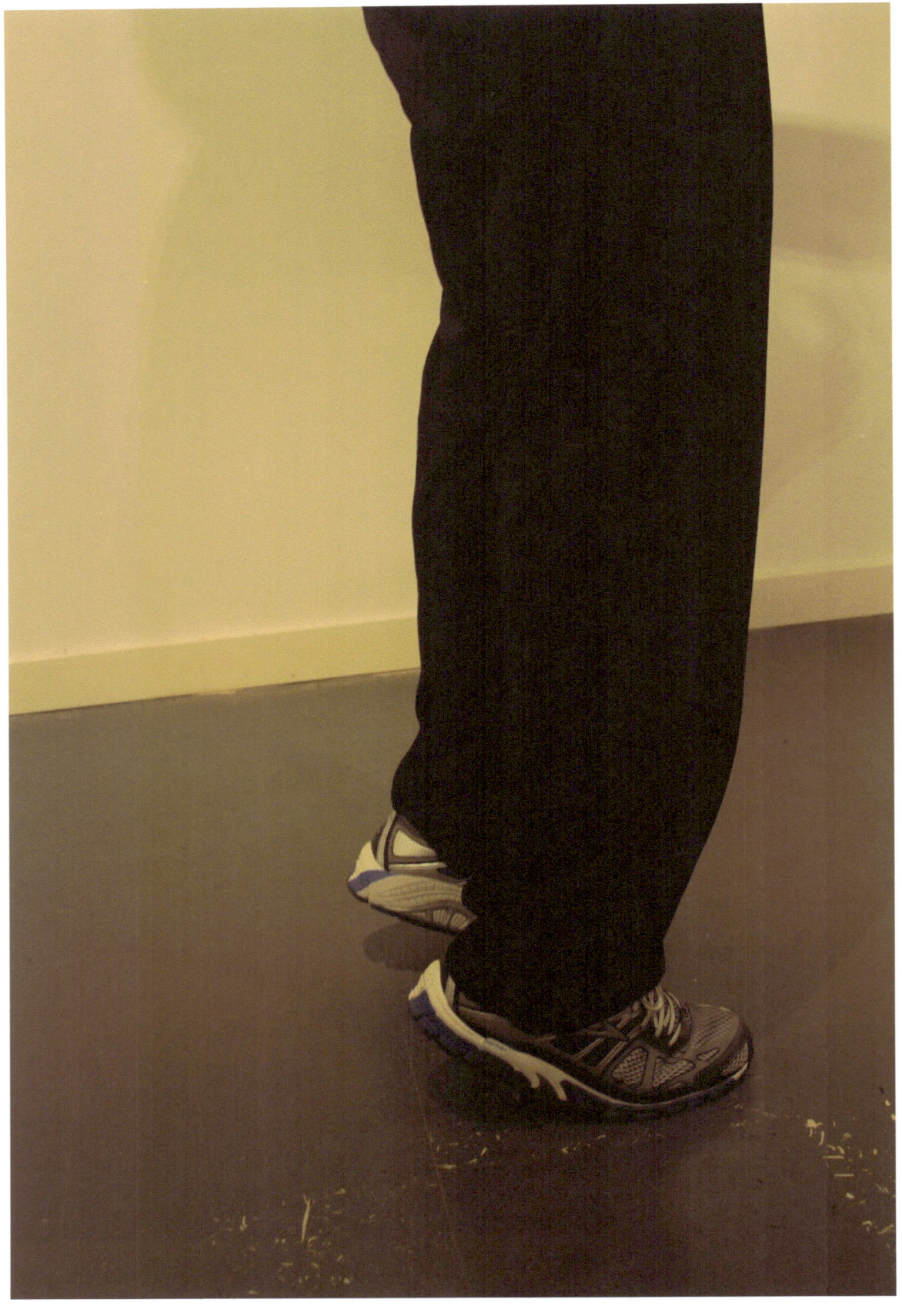

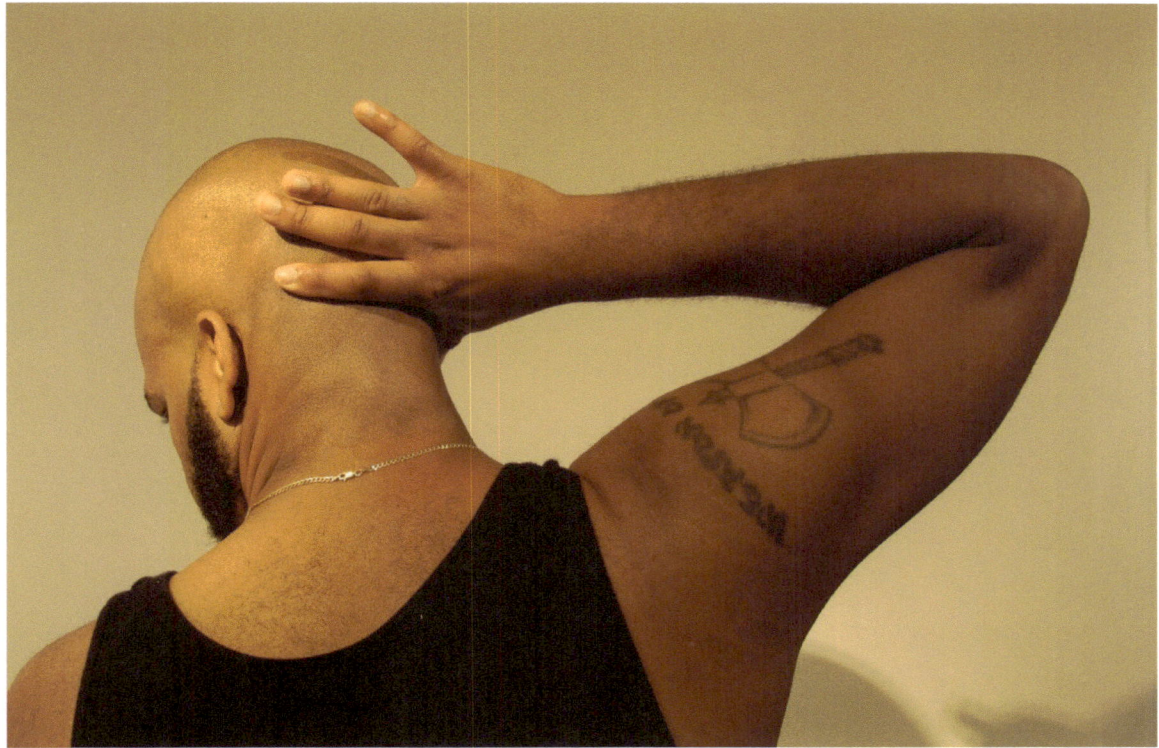

Hook raise

Stretch pulling one arm behind back,
Clasping hand behind your back,

Shrugs

Arm lifts (front > side),
Circles forward and backwards,
Triceps stretch across chest,
Triceps stretch above head,

Hands

Rotate wrist clockwise and counter clockwise (Normal and Fast)
Twist wrist from left to right, fast,
Flap wrist up and down, fast,
Back of hands clasping in center bring up to chest,

Weighted Tilts

Bend middle finger back up and down,
Stretch open palms,

Abs and Back
Lean sideways,

Turn left to right,
Bend over to touch toes,
Bend over to left and right legs, in order

CUTTING

Cutting

Cutting is the work that defines a barber, not conversing, managing, marketing or anything else. Know and love your work. This section will provide you with a wealth of information on cutting and its techniques. Below is an example of a good cutting.

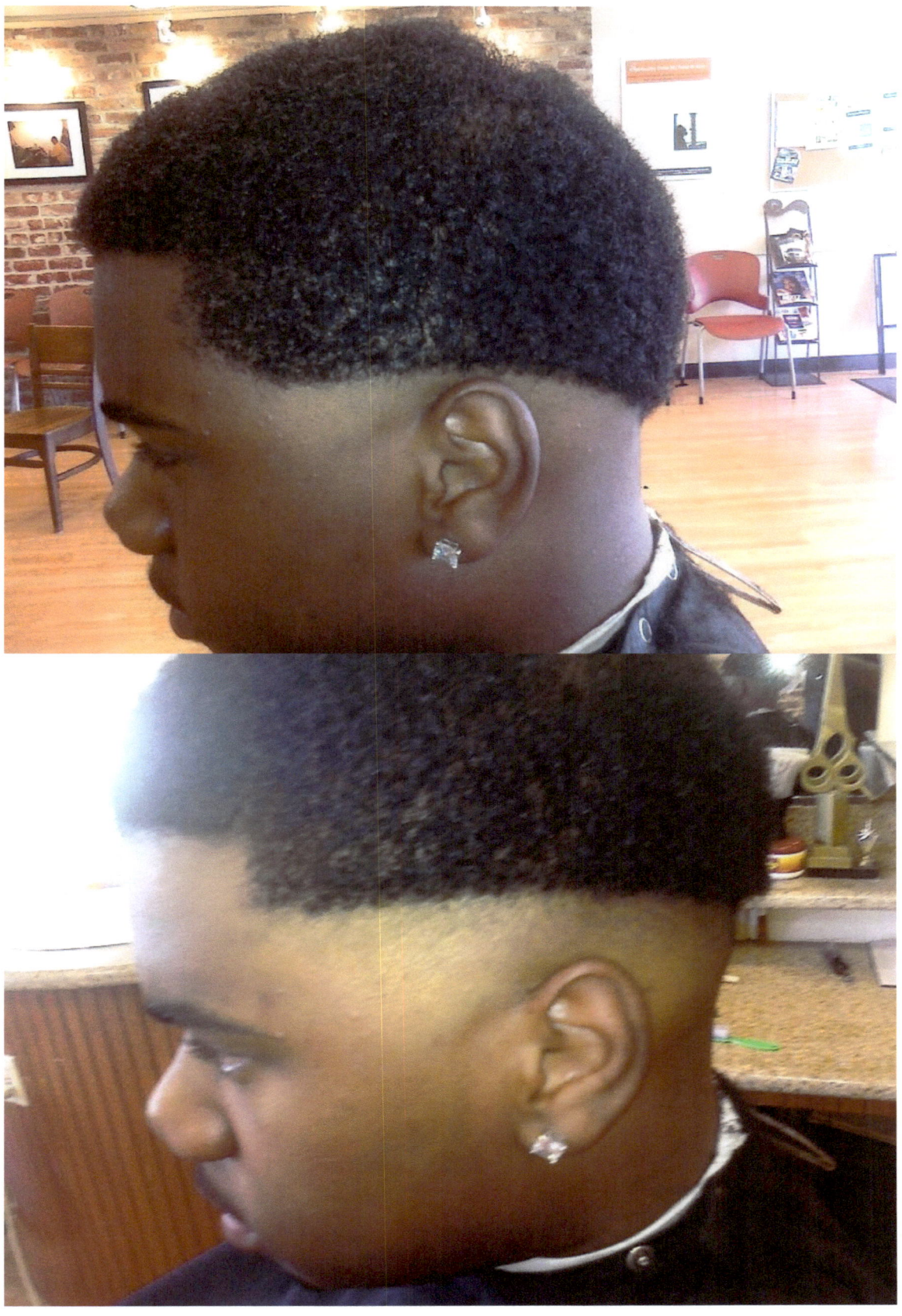

Blade Theory

Blade theory is a structured way of cutting hair. This easy step by step method will help in most situations. You will understand what professional blades and guards can do. Knowledge that will help develop the vision to create a great haircut, as well as giving a blue print that is easy to follow.

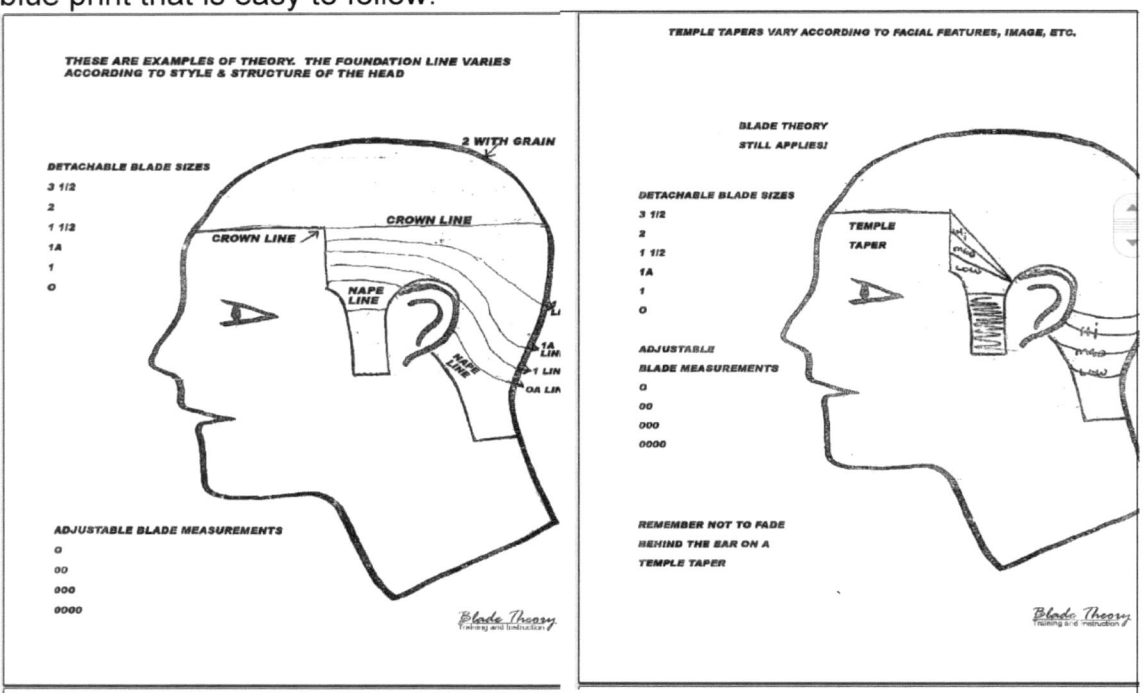

Blades and Guards:
Detachable Blades – Guard equivalent
00000-Trimmer
000-adjustables close
0A- adjustable open half way
Adjustable open
00(guard) adjustable closed
½ -00(guard) adjustable open half way
2-0(guard) adjustable closed
½-0A (guard) adjustable closed

Principle
When cutting against the grain, you will cut lower and even. Cutting with the grain leaves hair
Longer, great for creating a smoother finish.

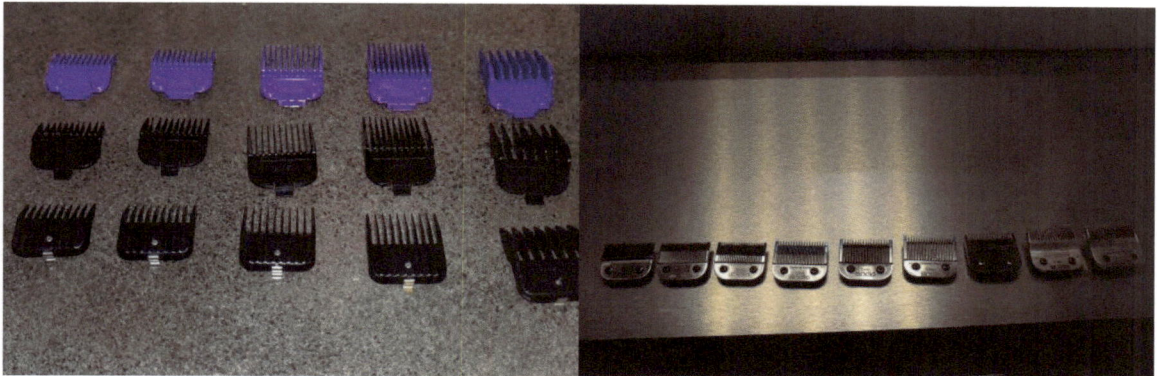

Against the Grain = With the Grain

1 against = 0A with
1A against = 1 with (best to use adjustable clipper depending on hair texture)
1 ½ against = 1a with (some textures will call for 1)
2 against = 1 ½ with
3 ½ against = 2 with.

Technique: Create uniformity. Allow for even spacing in your blade progression to create the most balanced outcome. **PAY** attention to head shape and contours. Apply scooping technique to establish smooth blended blade progression. Become familiar with using your mirror. The mirror will help you stay consistent, identify shadows and dark areas.

To eliminate shadows, first go over shadow section with the blade that was initially used in that section. If no results show, adjust to a lower blade level until you reach the desired result. Result should be a smooth even blend.

Tip for eliminating lines in haircut: Whatever blade that was used to create the line will be the same blade used to eliminate the line. Practicing the scooping technique will help.

Fading

Fading is a series of creating levels over progressive lengths and then blending that length into the next length by using a slight scooping motion.

Whatever length you use with the grain it equivalent length is 1 ½ to 2 steps longer against the grain.

You can use a 1 ½ against the grain and comeback with the grain with a one blade and have a smooth even cut without creating a patch. This principle applies if you go longer or shorter lengths.

6 step fade

1. Top length 1 ½
2. below top 1a
3. below 1
4. below 0A
5. below 000
6. below 00000 or Bald

Tips
- Change hands for proper ergonomics
- Avoid using awkward cutting motions that can lead to joint pain over time

Blending

By learning to cut with blades you'll have develop a great understanding of blending hair of various lengths and style. This will be of great benefit with fading all textures of hair. By having this understanding and skill, your speed will greatly increase as well as helping you develop an even better understanding and use of adjustable clippers.

Beards

Objective
To take facial hair and give it uniformity and precision. Highlight certain dominant features and give balance to weaker ones.

Types of Beards
Full beard, medium beard (balanced mid-way on the cheek, parallel to the corners of the mouth) low beard (balance on the jaw or mandible bone). Goatees and side burns.

Principals
Sides should be identical. (Before starting, examine how much hair is present. It will assist you in creating boundaries and balance). Fullness of the face is important. Fuller

faces, aim to give balance when lining the cheeks. It will open up the face and draw more attention to the eyes.
When the neck is also full find a good mid-point under the jaw or mandible bone slightly above the Adams apple. It will hide any flabby areas. Work with the features they already have. Ones with sharp or pointed features look good with facial hair with the same consistency. The same with rounded features.

Starting
Create lines that will act as boundaries. Vertical line closet to the ear down to the jaw or mandible bone. Next a horizontal line under the mandible. Shave all hair on the neck below this line. Determine the appropriate width on the beard itself. It will vary with style. Mustache balance length by using the length of the mouth, with or narrowness of the chin. Distance from top lip to nose, and fullness of the lips. Lightly line the hair on the top lip that may be hanging over. Line top of the lip according to client preference.

The Art of Lining

Observation
Individuals have many unique facial features and head structures. The goal is to frame their face, to give a look of precision, while using the most outer perimeter of hair possible. In some cases, there will be lines that you will have to create to achieve a balance and precise look.

Tip
Avoid the headache and consult with your client. Show them the mirror and explain your plan, and thoughts. You may find some valuable info about your client's preferences. They'll appreciate the consideration.

Tools: comb, Liners

Outlining the outermost perimeter of hair.

What to look for

Outer most hair on face and nape. It will vary from one side of the head to the other. Use points of references.

Nape area

Lining behind the ears should be kept low, go higher to show more Definition: Remember, check with your client whenever there is a time you are considering going past their natural perimeter. Follow that principle to establish a straight line on the nape area.

Face

The front line should respect the natural hair line as much as possible. The line you make frames the face, be balanced, and have a look of precision. Use eyebrows and facial features to establish where points of reference along the eyebrow should be. Use a comb to lay hair down around the hair line. Cut balance horizontal lines that will act like a traveling guide line across the forehead.

Vertical Lines on the Profile

(Note: the point where all lines intersect, create sharp corners and edges, to add more detail to your frame.) Lines should give the illusion of being straight. Pay attention to the angle of which you make your lines. Maintain identical angles on each side of the head. Your creativity will assist you when facing more challenging situations.

Arch and side burns: Goal is to frame the eyebrows and best captures your client's style. Use straight lines at the top and bottom part of your arc. Those lines will set the perimeter for you to create your arc. Distance from eyes to ears can vary, along with the presence of hair. Balance each sides, so it compliments their features.

Frequently Asked Questions

Q: I cut the customer's hair at the length they request, but sometimes it won't lie down in the bang or crown when I am done. What am I doing wrong?

A: Sounds like the areas that you are having problems with are where hair swirls or cowlick. To get these levels even you must go against the grain in the direction of the swirl to get it even, then drop to a lower guard or blade and go with the grain to smooth out texture. If you are unsure what length to use, as a caution start out with your higher guards, trust your knowledge of blade progression. Cut till you see results.

Q: I always wet the hair before I cut, but I heard that there are some hair traits that I should cut dry. What are they and how do I cut dry hair?

A: Overly curly (black) hair should be cut dry, straighten hair when clipper cutting, wet when shear cutting.

Q: I've noticed that I can use the same clipper guard for the same haircut, but it looks shorter on some customers than others. Why is that?

A: Texture and density is different for every client, never assume the same guard will perform the same way for everyone. Note that density, texture, and direction can and does vary on different areas of the client's head. Always start off with a higher guard first and analyze how hair reacts and looks. Remember comb hair with the grain and cut against.

Q: It seems like I frequently end up with lines when I blend different lengths of hair. How can I get rid of these?

A: I recommend leaving lines in the head as you climb up your blade progression, your problem is technique, and better scooping motion will eliminate this problem

The End

So you made it to the end! Take what knowledge is in this book along with your passion and be a great barber to someone. Value yourself and value others as much as possible. Be persistent, aggressive, and continuously take action. Quiet the voices of negativity in and around you. Never speak negatively about what you love and success; real success will always be yours.

For more amazing resources visit www.betheworldsgreatestbarber.com

BARBER WANTED

JOB DESCRIPTION:
Barber needed to provide *great* services. Must listen extremely well and always speak from the heart. Barber will take on rolls as trusted adviser on various areas of my life; such as, fashion, career, family, relationships, education, and following my dreams.

Barber must have a positive outlook on life and care enough to tell me I was wrong. Must be willing to share life experiences so I may grow and avoid similar mistakes. Need barber to never judge me for my thoughts or actions and actively try to bring out the best in me visually through his haircuts and the best in my character through his words.

Barber must challenge me to dream big and pursue my dreams. Barber must do or have done the same for himself.

Travel:
Barber will be required on occasion to go to birthday parties, graduations, weddings, funerals, sporting events, and much more.
Barber must take his business seriously and avoid doing anything harmful through words or actions that may compromise our safety,

Benefits
Love
Sharing life with amazing people
Fulfillment

REFERENCES

Algra, Bruce, Bruce Algra's First Aid Series. www.algra.com/first-aid-posters

Brunson, Russell, Dotcom Secrets. New York: Morgan James Publishing © 2015

Buffini Brian, Peak Producers. Buffini & Company, Carlsbad CA, www.buffiniandcompany.com 2015

Carnegie, Dale, Rev. ed How To Win Friends & Influence People. New York: Simon and Schuster, ©1981.

Carter, Wanda. To Achieve Your Dreams Remember Your ABC's

Clason, George, The Richest Man in Babylon. New York: Penguin Books © 1924

www.compliancesigns.com

Cotti Gregory, 15 Customer Service Skills That Every Employee Needs, www.helpscout.net. 2/20/2013

De Cima, Jay, Fixer Jay's Real Estate Investor Training Seminar. Redding CA: KJAY Publishing © 2010

Fletcher, Bryant, Blade Theory. Washington Dc. 2003

Ferris, Timothy, The 4-Hour Body. New York: Penguin Random House LLC. © 2007, 2009

Ferris, Timothy, The 4-Hour Work Week. New York: Penguin Random House LLC. © 2007, 2009

Gerber, Michael, E-myth Revisited. New York: Harper Collins©1995

Hicks, Esther and Jerry, Ask And It is Given. Carlsbad California: Hay House Inc.© 2004

Hill, Napoleon, The Laws of Success. Meriden, Conn: The Ralston University Press. © 1928

WWW.INVESTOPEDIA.COM

Keller, Gary, The Millionaire Real Estate Agent. New York: McGowan-Hill. ©2004

Klos Jo, Gates Carla, 10 Ways To Exceed Expectations In Customer Service, http://blog.glance.net. 02/23/2010

Solomon Micah. 10 Trending Changes In Customers And In Customer Service Expectations. www.forbes.com 08/08/2014

Stanley, Thomas, and William Danko. The Millionaire Next Door. New York: Pocket Books 1996.

WWW.TDAMERITRADE.COM

In loving memory of Leon and Opal Whitmore, Bryant Fletcher, Mr. Charles, Mr. Hutchinson, Pastor, Mr. Ray

www.ingramcontent.com/pod-product-compliance
Lightning Source LLC
Chambersburg PA
CBHW041540220426
43664CB00002B/15